THE PSY(
RESEARCH C

The Psychology Research Companion: Fron. ~~ct *to working life*
not only gives you the skills and confiden ᴊnduct your psychology research project at university but also is ᴜᴇ first book to show how
these skills will help you get ahead in your first job in the workplace.

Jessica S. Horst, an American psychologist teaching in the UK, takes
you through every step of the research process: from conceiving your
research question and choosing a research methodology to organizing
your time and resources effectively. The book includes sections on ethics, data management, working with research participants and report
writing, but each chapter is also informed by the wider aim of providing
a toolkit for working life. Each chapter is packed with tips and skills that
can be taken into the workplace, including working collaboratively and
organising your workload, as well as discussing your research project in
interview situations and when applying for jobs.

This invaluable guide will appeal to all undergraduate and postgraduate
psychology students whose aim is to learn a set of transferable research
skills as well as to obtain a good degree result.

Jessica S. Horst is a faculty member at the University of Sussex, UK. She
has won a teaching award for her supervision of psychology research
projects and also received a number of awards for her own research,
including the American Psychological Association Dissertation Award
in Developmental Psychology.

The Psychology Research Companion

From student project to working life

Jessica S. Horst

Routledge
Taylor & Francis Group

LONDON AND NEW YORK

First published 2016
2 Park Square, Milton Park, Abingdon, Oxon OX14 4RN

and by Routledge
711 Third Avenue, New York, NY 10017

Routledge is an imprint of the Taylor & Francis Group, an informa business

British Library Cataloguing in Publication Data
A catalogue record for this book is available from the British Library

Library of Congress Cataloging-in-Publication Data
Horst, Jessica S.
   The psychology research companion : from student project to working life / Jessica S. Horst. — 1st Edition.
      pages cm
   Includes bibliographical references.
   1. Psychology—Research.   I. Title.
   BF76.5.H664 2015
   150.72—dc23
   2015010237

ISBN: 978-1-138-78531-1 (hbk)
ISBN: 978-1-138-78532-8 (pbk)
ISBN: 978-1-315-76791-8 (ebk)

Typeset in Palatino
by Apex CoVantage, LLC

MIX
Paper from responsible sources
FSC® C013604

Printed and bound by CPI Group (UK) Ltd, Croydon, CR0 4YY

To James

Contents

Figures

Tables

Acknowledgements

First, I would like to thank my wonderful husband, Ryan, who has been so very supportive during this project, as he is with every aspect of my career and home life. I am also grateful to my editor, Russell George. I would also like to thank Martina Micaletto for her editorial assistance and Libby Volke and her colleagues at Routledge.

I am thankful for the comments and helpful suggestions provided by Camilla Batchelor, Kelly Campbell, Zoe Flack, Matt Hilton, Sam Ranson and Emilly Scott. I'm grateful for the encouragement I received from my parents and my work colleagues and friends, in particular Sophie Forster, Sarah King, Kristine Kovack-Lesh, Eisuke Koya, Eleanor Miles, Bonny Oliver, Alison Pike, Adele Seelke and Vanessa Simmering.

Finally, I would like to thank my students who provided comments for this book and the students I have worked with or advised who inspired me to write a book on this topic.

Thank you, everyone.

1 Introduction and starting out

You may or may not continue to do research in psychology – and that's OK. Fortunately, a lot of the skills you will learn by doing research are transferable: you can apply these skills to the next thing you do. Sometimes it may not seem immediately apparent how these skills are transferable or how you might spin them to answer a question in a job interview. I'm hoping that after you read this book, the transferability and marketability of these skills will be much clearer. Along the way I hope to give you tips and advice to help you hone these skills so you can do your research (and your next job) to the best of your ability.

This is a book about transferable skills

This book is not meant to be a statistics textbook, an overview of the best empirical research methods out there or a complete guide on how to write academic articles well. There are already some excellent books on those topics – and I list some recommendations at the end of this chapter. This book is meant to be a companion to help you with *the other aspects* of conducting psychology research, from actually recruiting participants to data entry to organizing the big stack of journal articles you will read. My goal is to help you with these aspects while showing you how you aren't just doing busywork: these aspects of your research are teaching you transferable skills that you can use later, whether or not you continue doing psychology research. There are a couple of chapters on writing and presenting data, but that's because clear writing and data presentation are important transferable skills.

I have asked former students about how they have used the skills they learned doing undergraduate and masters-level psychology research after they graduated. I have included these comments to show you the wide range of jobs in which you can apply these transferable skills. Some of these former students also provided other helpful tips for you.

"A final year project is not just something that has to be done because your university tells you to do one. It is an important piece of research that can help you make important steps in your pursuit of a career."

—Camilla, BSc
Assistant Psychologist
(National Health Service)

I have also included some information that you might be too timid to ask someone about in real life, because it is a "dumb question." I once took a very challenging class and heard myself ask questions every week that started with "this might be a dumb question . . ." or "maybe I'm not getting this, but . . ." I really thought it was just me. Then, several weeks later, one of my classmates confided in me: "I'm so glad you always ask questions. I have a lot of the same questions, but I don't want to ask them in case it's just me [not understanding]." After that I realized that if one person has a question, it's likely that many others have the same question but just aren't asking it. As you read this book, there may be times when you see a paragraph answering a question you don't need answered (either because you have already learned that tidbit or because it doesn't apply to the kind of research you do): just move on to the next paragraph, but know I've included that information for the reader who may be too timid to ask someone about it in real life.

If you do feel like you have a lot of dumb questions: first, believe me that this is normal. It really is. (You can even look up "imposter syndrome" to see how common it is.) Second, keep in mind that if you already knew everything, you would already have the degree you are working toward: you are *supposed to* be learning, and you are *supposed to* not yet know everything – and quite honestly, even people who already have degrees are still learning and also don't know everything! You might even consider yourself to be in good company: Socrates, a pivotal figure in the history of philosophy, is famous for saying, "I know that I do not know" (Plato/Fowler, 1995). Finally, keep in mind that there are people you can talk to about specific advice, including your supervisor, other lab members and peers, as well as your campus writing center if you have one.

"This may be the first time you are collecting data, speaking to participants and actually running a study. It's fine to be nervous in this situation. Your confidence will develop with time. You shouldn't think you aren't doing a good job just because you're nervous or under-confident about doing something for the first time."

—Naureen, BSc
Education Center Manager

Structure of the book

I've tried to write this book so you can either read it in order or dip in and out of it when you want more information about something as you encounter it. To this end, I've ordered the chapters to cover the research tasks and skills in the order most students will encounter them, but I've also tried to use meaningful and memorable subheadings so you can find things you may want to wait to read later when you really need them.

Box 1.1: Phases to a research project

Your project will advance through several phases, which are roughly:

1. Getting the go-ahead (finding a supervisor/mentor, getting permission to do a project)
2. Planning (designing the study and obtaining ethical approval)
3. Data collection
4. Data analysis
5. Writing and presenting (although you can write some sections earlier)

This introductory chapter covers the things you may want to know before you begin and includes my comprehensive research project checklist.

The next two chapters cover the day-to-day stuff for actually starting a study and collecting data (Chapter 2: All in a day's work) and managing your time (Chapter 3: All in good time [management]). The time management chapter follows the data collection chapter because it is often not until students really get going that they begin to wonder if they are using their time well. However, read them in the order you think is best for you. The daily work and time management skills covered in these chapters may serve you very well after you graduate.

The next chapter (Chapter 4: Make your computer work for you) covers computer skills that aren't usually taught in classes. It's about clever ways to get the computer to work harder so you don't have to. This will free up more of your time and mental energy for the things your computer can't do (like explain how your data provides evidence supporting Theory X). So, on some level this chapter is also about time management.

The final two chapters cover writing (Chapter 5: The write way) and presenting your work (Chapter 6: Presenting your findings). The writing chapter includes useful phrases and real examples of how to make your writing clear and concise. The final chapter covers figures, tables, presentations and interviews.

Box 1.2: Terminology in this book

Different departments and programs sometimes have different names for the same things. Here are the terms I'll use throughout the book:

- **Project,** also known as, Senior Project, Capstone Project, Experiment, Study, etc.
- **Dissertation**, also known as, Project Paper, Research Paper, Thesis, Honor's Thesis, etc.
- **Mentor and supervisor** are used interchangeably because the faculty member assigned to work with you should serve as both a mentor and a supervisor. Also, "mentor" is more widely used in the United States and "supervisor" in the UK. Some departments use advisor, and you may also hear principal investigator (PI, the faculty member or post-doc who is ultimately in charge of the project and likely earned external funding for it).
- **Ethics Committee**, also known as Human Subjects Committee, Institutional Review Board (IRB), etc.

Throughout this book you will also find both American and British terminology. I've written this book to contain advice for both North American- and European-style universities. I know firsthand what's involved in student research on both sides of the Atlantic because I was a student and grad student in the United States, and I am a faculty member in the UK. Where the terms/phrases differ dramatically I'll use both forms, e.g. "page protectors (document wallets)."

Pick and choose

You likely have a lot of choices ahead of you, ranging from choosing a mentor and topic to choosing your method to choosing which colors to use in your figures. Whether you choose your project supervisor/ mentor or topic first will depend on the spread of research interests in your department and how much thought you have already put into your research project topic.

- If you have narrowed your interests down to a (general) area of psychology (e.g. social psychology, unconscious bias research, etc.), you may want to find a mentor and then hone in on the exact topic.
- If you already have a research question in mind, you may want to approach the faculty in that broad area or who do research on that topic (topic → mentor).

Choosing a supervisor and mentor

Choosing who will supervise your project is one of the biggest decisions you will make about your research. You want to choose a mentor whose supervision style and personality work well with your own and who conducts research in a general area you find interesting. The most common way to choose a supervisor is to consider which classes you have enjoyed most and then approach the faculty who taught those classes and topics.

Some faculty are very hands-on and approach student projects as an active collaboration. Other faculty view the student research experience as an apprenticeship, where the goal is to impart their knowledge to the student until the student can work independently (in so far as scientists work independently). With this style you might actually work under a PhD student or post-doc. And other faculty are very hands-off and consider student projects as a chance for students to demonstrate what they have already learned. You should think about what style of mentorship and supervision will be most beneficial for you and aim to find a mentor who has that approach (though often you can speak up and say, "I need more guidance" or "I want to first try this part independently" as your project progresses).

One thing you will want to consider is how busy the potential supervisor is. It is easy to see how much time faculty members spend in lectures, but it's harder to see how many other preexisting commitments they have (e.g. editing journals, writing grants, etc.). Just because people are busy or famous doesn't mean they won't be outstanding mentors, but you want to ensure you have the same expectations. It is very awkward if a student expects to work closely with a faculty member for several hours per week but finds that most of the guidance is coming from a PhD student and the official faculty mentor only checks in every other week. The student may still be getting great mentorship and supervision; it's just not what the student originally envisioned. Some departments have policies and guidelines for how much time you can expect your supervisor to spend with you. Some faculty also have their own habits (e.g. my undergraduate mentor met with me once each week for one hour). When you approach potential faculty mentors, ask how much time they typically spend with their research students. If they do not know, try to ask one of their current or former research students.

"There are many different kinds of supervisors out there, and choosing one on the basis of how you want to be supervised is very important. Some of my friends chose their mentors on the basis that they were a 'big name' in the field but not on the number of contact hours they would have. For me, I learned that I can work relatively independently but that I need guidance and support at regular intervals. I also learned that it was important for me to have a supervisor who valued my thoughts and ideas as a scientist. This gave me a real boost in being more confident in my work, and in the long run, allowed me to become more independent. I simply wouldn't work well with a supervisor who was too busy being famous and traveling the world but had no time to reply to emails or arrange meetings. Therefore, despite the fact that many students may consider it most important to be with a 'big name' and not to care too much about contact hours, I know this wouldn't work for me."

—Lauren H., BSc
PhD Student

Keep in mind that your choice in supervisor might influence what kind of study you can do. For example, some faculty only allow students to work on preexisting projects or do secondary data analysis (see Greenhoot & Dowsett, 2012 for additional advice on secondary data analysis). Bettmann (2009) has a useful article on choosing a mentor, though it is not written for undergraduate psychology students (but see Foreshaw, 2013).

Tip: Volunteer

Where possible, try to gain experience as a voluntary research assistant before the start of your project. This will enable you to get to know your mentor and the rest of the lab group (if applicable) and possibly get training on the methods you will be using. This can be especially useful if you will be using methods you have not experienced as a research participant during your intro psychology class.

Choosing a topic

Your *specific* research topic doesn't *really* matter. It's kind of like choosing which movie to go to on a date: the point is to get the experience. As long as you don't make a really bad choice (for example seeing a gross-out comedy when your date is in the mood for a period drama), you should be fine. So, for example, if you narrow down that you want to do a project within social psychology, the exact topic isn't really the point – the point is to learn how to do social psychology research and gain hands-on experience with the methods. These are transferable skills, which you can transfer to another job after graduation or you can apply to future research based on your understanding of the literature and on your sense for what kinds of experiments work. Most PhD students and faculty are actually working on research that is a few degrees apart from their original interests. You can also see this among historic psychology figures (e.g. Piaget, Pavlov).

Of course, you should still care about your *general* topic. It will make the experience much more fun, especially if your research project is a requirement.

"If you don't find the topic particularly interesting, it goes without saying that writing the dissertation will feel much more of a chore. Do your research and read up on the faculty member's research interests and pick the research, which jumps out at you."

—Sam, BSc
Life Skills Recovery Worker (NHS)

So, how do you decide which topic to choose? You might choose something you are interested in because of your own previous history (see Field & Hole, 2003). For example, if you grew up with a single parent perhaps you are interested in how children from single- and dual-parent families differ in their sense of responsibility or autonomy. Perhaps you have viewed various behavior in public or on television and you want to get to understand why regular people behave in certain ways (for more on finding inspiration this way, see Foreshaw, 2013).

Another approach is to consider if you have read an article and think there is something to add to the story. Perhaps you have another explanation for a finding or you feel passionately that there was a flaw in a study that you can correct. Do note, however, that if you go this route, you may need to replicate the original study or at least one of the conditions in the original study. This can be problematic (see Box 2.6). There are many reasons why replication attempts sometimes fail. Try to have a plan in mind of how you will proceed if you fail to replicate the original. When at all possible, use methods that your mentor has already used to help increase your likelihood of success.

Finally, if you don't know where to begin, ask your mentor about the current studies the lab is running and what might be next. You can often work on a study the lab would be running anyway – in fact, for students doing research in labs that involve nonhuman participants (mice, rats, pigeons, etc.), this is often the norm. There may be a couple of projects that you can choose from. Sometimes this approach worries students and can be seen as less than ideal because most students want to think that the study was their own idea. But there are several big advantages. First, there are likely to be really good resources available. Second, the mentor and other lab members (PhD students, post-docs) have likely used this method before and can answer a lot of the logistical questions. In addition, these people likely have a good list of papers to get you started on reading relevant material. But the biggest advantage is that your mentor will really care about your study and want to see it succeed. This will increase his or her motivation to meet with you about the study and ensure that your study stays on track time-wise and you always have all of the resources you need. If you are still concerned about the original idea aspect, keep in mind that you can bring in your own ideas and creativity in your introduction and discussion. Perhaps by the time you write the discussion you will have lots of ideas about practical implications that you can use to show your contribution to the project.

Feasibility

Sometimes a potential mentor may try to steer you away from a particular topic or research question. Assume this person actually has your best interests in mind. Some topics are very interesting but not feasible in the relatively short time frame you have (especially when you take into account that you may be waiting a while for ethical approval). For example, it may not be possible to recruit a large enough sample of number-synesthetes or you may not have enough time to follow-up and re-interview your participants six months after they have moved in together. There may also be ethical considerations you haven't thought of that the potential mentor knows about.

If this happens ask yourself what the *real* question you are after is. For example, I had a student once approach me about doing a project on how nursery rhymes can help children remember things. At the time I didn't know anything about nursery rhymes through research (just what I knew from my own childhood and babysitting). So I asked what she was really after, and we agreed to do a project exploring whether the kind of verbal input children receive helps them learn (in this case children were read a storybook that either rhymed or didn't rhyme). The student ended up having a lot of fun creating her own materials, and the study worked well (and she also earned top marks).

Thinking about feasibility isn't only a question about recruitment and time frame. You also want to consider how you will analyze the data. What will you report? Can you obtain data you can quantify or qualitative data that you can report well? Here your mentor will be especially important. Ask your mentor to look at your idea and design and check if it looks like you can feasibly analyze it. The last thing you want is to spend months working on a project only to discover that no one (not even your mentor) knows how to analyze the kind of data you collected or that you forgot to add a baseline so there is nothing to compare against.

Box 1.3: Qualitative research

Not all student research projects are quantitative. Depending on the questions you want to answer with your research project, your study might be better suited for a qualitative approach where you interview participants and transcribe their narratives or you give participants an open-ended questionnaire and analyze their responses. There are many different ways to code qualitative data (for lengthier discussions see Foreshaw, 2013; Wood et al., 2012).

This freedom makes such projects both highly creative and also challenging. Although most of the examples in this book are quantitative, students who conduct qualitative research are also learning the same transferable skills, such as record keeping, time management, using Word, giving presentations, etc. In addition, by analyzing qualitative data you will gain skills that can be applied to understanding comments from focus groups, responses about your next company on social media and trends in customer reviews for your company's product or your hospital's facilities.

Research with other populations

You may have heard the term *opportunity sample*, which refers to how easy it is to complete research with undergraduate students as research participants, relative to conducting research with other populations. If you are interested in research with other populations (children, nonhuman animals, stroke patients, etc.), find a mentor who works with that population.

You wouldn't come to me and say, "I really like your approach to understanding how children learn the meanings of words. I want to study how chimpanzees learn the meanings of words." So why would you go to someone who studies a topic you are interested in and ask him or her to supervise a study about that topic with preschoolers?

Box 1.4: Conducting research with children

Children are considered a vulnerable population according to the APA and BPS. You may need a legal background check before you may conduct research with children, and it can sometimes take weeks or months for the paperwork to come back. (Perhaps you can do this the spring before you start your project.) Someone on the ethics committee for your department should be able to advise you on how to get started.

It is extremely rewarding to conduct research with children – you really get to show off your creativity when designing tasks and materials. But there are trade-offs. It is more difficult to find and recruit child participants relative to adult participants. Children also cannot sit and complete a study for as long as adults can, so you may need to reconsider your task or have your participants complete the task across more than one day. There are also scheduling issues because you may need to work around nap times, school holidays and the schedules of families where all of the parents work full-time.

You will need to be very flexible with your time so that you can offer decent times for sessions to families (remember they aren't on campus and cannot just swing by the lab after a 12:00 class). Most children wake up much earlier than students (e.g. 6:00 or 7:00). But 9:00 many parents feel like it's the middle of the morning and a great time to come do a study. Do take parents' suggestions of when to schedule a session into account – no parent wants to be embarrassed by a crying, tired child trying to complete an experiment, so parents will generally suggest times when their children are alert and not overly tired. If you are testing in schools, you may also be given set days when you can and cannot test the children so that your study does not interfere with the children's curriculum (for further discussion about testing in schools, see Wood, Giles, & Percy, 2012).

If you are really interested in one topic in a special population and you know one person who researches that topic but another person who works with that population, consider if you can be co-supervised by two mentors. Even if you have two mentors, however, you will want to list a primary mentor for your paperwork. Coming from experience, I recommend listing the person who will be most involved with the day-to-day aspects as the primary mentor because this person will have to help you gain access to your population and handle resources (e.g. participant reimbursement, ordering food for animals). This person will also have a better idea of how to write a successful ethics application for your study. This is just the easiest set-up; it doesn't mean you won't discuss the exciting theoretical implications with the co-mentor!

Warning! If you conduct a project on a nonopportunity sample, it will likely take you longer to collect your data than it will take your friends whose student participants are completing questionnaires. This is totally OK, but I want you to know this so you are not taken aback when others come to you when you are still piloting and tell you they are already finished. That kind of awkward conversation can feel a bit depressing, but keep your eye on the ball: remember why you feel passionately about your topic and how excited you are that you get to conduct a challenging study because you really care about your population.

Box 1.5: Conducting "very technical" research

You may be interested in conducting research with a nonhuman population (e.g. mice, rats) or with patients and their respective control group. Some of this research is behavioral, but other research involves fMRI, fancy microscopes and other expensive equipment. In such labs you may first be told to shadow a more senior lab member (e.g. a PhD student or post-doc) who will train you on some of the techniques you will need as you help pitch in with other less-glamorous jobs that need doing in the lab. In some cases, for insurance and health and safety reasons you will always work alongside someone when you are in the lab. Such highly technical research is exceptionally expensive, and such labs often cannot supervise undergraduate experiments that do not contribute to the lab's overall research program (read: the research projects that make the lab financially feasible). As your skills improve from assisting another lab member, you may then be allowed to take more of the lead on some research the lab is doing (e.g. your project might involve one experiment that is part of a multi-experiment project on the faculty member's grant).

Ethical approval

You (or your mentor) must obtain ethical approval before you may really begin working on your project. There are plenty of things you can do while you wait for the paperwork (see checklist at the end of this chapter), but recruiting and testing participants *must not* be one of them.

Just like writing a paper, a great way to get an idea of what to do is to look at someone else's successful version. Hopefully someone in your lab group will have a successful ethical application to show you. This is the best place to start looking because that application will have been sent to the same ethics committee (though some members and policies may have changed in the meantime) and it will likely include the same methods.

If you have consent forms from when you participated in studies, you can also use those as examples. Once I helped a student submit an application for a study that required some deception (if we had told the participants the real reason for the task, there was very good reason to expect it would change how they behaved). In this case we found it helpful to talk to others in the department who used deception and to the chair of our ethics committee before we submitted our application.

Tip: Submit early

It can take a long time to write a good ethics application and you shouldn't rush that process, but you should start early. Often ethics committees review applications in the order they are received, so the earlier you submit yours, the sooner it will be reviewed. For some committees you can expect a prompt turnaround, but for others you can expect to wait months (not a typo). Your mentor and others in your department will know the general timeline to expect with your committee.

Expect your ethics committee to send your application back to you requesting some revision. You might need to change some wording on the consent form so it is less ambiguous or you might need to specify some detail of your task. The more detail you can provide in your original submission the better. I also find it helpful to cite published studies that use the same methods whenever possible.

However, there is such a thing as putting in too much detail. If you specify you want to present exactly N trials and later want to add two more trials, you will need to submit a revision of your application to your committee. You may want to specify "approximately N trials" and a general timeframe (e.g. "The entire task should take no more than fifteen minutes to complete.").

I would be very surprised if you haven't been taught about ethics in psychology already. You may have even completed a test or certificate to demonstrate you understand psychological ethical considerations. You should know that participation in experiments should always be voluntary. Human participants should either provide information consent or in the case of children, assent and have a parent or guardian provide informed consent. Your confidential records should be securely maintained. Participants should not suffer harm from being in the study. And participants (both human and non) should be well-treated.

A big part of the ethics application process is to ensure that you have systems in place to achieve these things. The ethics committee will look to see that your methods are reasonable and not harmful. Often at least one member of the ethics committee is a non-academic. This person may not have a degree in psychology, so you will want to explain how and why you plan to do all you plan to do as if you are writing for this person and trying to convince this person (the psychologists and other scientists on the committee will also understand your application if you write it this way). Keep in mind that you will need to explain and justify all of your methods (read: even recruiting participants or housing animals) not just the methods you use in your actual experiment.

For a discussion of the difference between confidentiality and anonymity, see Box 2.7 (p. 51).

Science is collaborative: working with other people

Psychology is a science and science is collaborative. Some mentors supervise students working in pairs or teams on the same project, and others supervise students each working on their own project. With either style you will need to work with your mentor and possibly interact with participants and others with whom you will share resources or from whom you will need help (e.g. the departmental administrator who disperses research funds).

> "I consider this to be one of the most important skills as in nearly every single job, getting along with colleagues is essential. In my case it is even more important as to be a good teacher you need to build good rapport with students in order to make sure both teacher and student are getting the most out of the class."
>
> —Anna, BSc
> English as a Second Language Teacher

The golden rule

When you are working with other people, the golden rule ("treat others as you would want to be treated") is oh so true. Let people you are meeting with know if you are running late, say "please" and "thank you" when you ask for favors (including thanking participants), leave the lab at least as clean and tidy as you found it, etc. These are small things, but they add up and signal to those you are working with that you respect them and their time.

"In terms of transferable skills I think one of the major ones is working in a small team and sharing the office/lab. This required quite a lot of organization and communication skills (and a good knowledge of Outlook!) for it to work effectively. This has been useful in all working environments I have experienced since. Especially my current work for the NHS!"

— Aislinn, BSc
Assistant Psychologist (National Health Service)

Handling conflicts

Preventing conflicts

Because science is so collaborative, you will be working with other people at some point. And when you work with people, there may be conflicts from time to time. Personally, I think the best skill I've honed for minimizing and avoiding conflicts is to communicate clearly – this can help stop misunderstandings before they happen. I try very hard to say what I mean. Often this requires being as specific as possible: from little things (e.g. "let's talk about this Tuesday after my 3:00 meeting" rather than the more common "let's talk about this Tuesday afternoon") to big things (e.g. "I'm worried that the project won't be finished on time if we continue at this rate of data collection" rather than the more vague "are we collecting data fast enough?" or "we still need a lot of participants").

Another way to avoid conflict is to keep everyone on a project updated if anything changes. This can be especially important if you make changes to a research project, because depending on what you said in your ethics application, you may need to submit a revision or addendum. Getting into the habit of keeping everyone on a project in the loop is also useful for avoiding hurt feelings (we're all real people, and no one likes feeling left out of important communications).

When conflict is unavoidable

Sometimes it's too late to go back and communicate more clearly or retroactively update someone on something. And sometimes it's not you, it's someone else who caused the conflict. What to do then?

If possible, speak to the other person directly, quickly and privately. If you wait, it is possible that when you finally talk about it you will be even more upset, because you've waited and the irritating behavior persisted, making you even more annoyed. If talking to the other person directly doesn't work, then speak with your faculty mentor. If your relationship with your mentor is the problem, then look through the materials you were given when you started your project and you should find your department's policies for where to go/what to do. If you find you want to change mentors and work with someone else, it is often possible to switch (but the sooner the better, so you have time to finish your project). Most faculty members understand when students want to switch and appreciate that some personality types work better together than others.

Sometimes you have no choice over who you have to work with. This can be true if you are doing a shared research project and can definitely be true when it comes to coworkers you might encounter after you graduate. Consider how long you will be working this closely with this person. Once testing or data analysis starts, can you work fairly independently of each other? Perhaps you can try not to spend a lot of time working at the same time as that person, especially alone. Another useful tactic is to consider how much you really need to share. If you are paired with another student on a study, consider which files and resources you can keep separate and keep as much separate as possible.

Perhaps you are working with someone who doesn't have the same level of attention to detail as you do. If he or she has even more attention to detail, that's great for you! But if he or she does not (e.g. typos on consent forms, inconsistent filing) take this ancient advice: pick your battles. Decide if it is really worth it to call attention to this person's mistakes (and if you must, try to do it privately). People don't like being told they are making mistakes – some people even get so defensive that they start to turn mean. But not all mistakes are equally destructive. Do you really need to mention the sloppy punctuation on the consent form? Can you just quietly fix it?

It is a shame that some people become so defensive when their mistakes are noticed. This is quite challenging in science fields because one thing scientists pride themselves on is identifying mistakes in other people's work or ways we can argue our own work is "better" (e.g. "Scarlett failed to account for this confound, therefore, in the current study, we . . ." or "However, Mustard's theory cannot account for why participants . . ."). But we all make mistakes. When someone notices a mistake you've made, the best things you can do are own up to it, be honest and try to fix it.

When I think of handling mistakes well, I often think of a research assistant of mine who accidentally deleted the only copy of some very important files (that's what happens when you re-format an external hard drive that still has files on it). It must have been difficult, but I have always respected how *she* came to me and was very straightforward when she said, "I made a mistake. I accidentally deleted those files. I am so sorry." I was so relieved that she hadn't hidden the mistake (e.g. putting off telling me until later as if it would rectify itself). And I respected her for being upfront and not using a lot of excuses. She could have easily tried to pass the blame by complaining "there was too much going on at once, how was I supposed to concentrate in such a noisy lab?" or "I was so tired because I'm working so hard here and I have another job too, you know." Of course, I learned something too: it was foolish of me not to have had an extra back-up method for files that were so important, which is why the lab now uses cloud services as an extra back-up method so this won't happen again.

Dissertation checklist

The following checklist can help you break your project and dissertation into more manageable steps. I've included a lot of small steps, but that's to help you hopefully avoid skipping a step and to help you achieve the thrill of checking something off your list! I've generally tried to put things in the order most people do them in, but your personal order may vary. In some cases I've put things earlier than some people do them so you can work more steadily and not have most of your work at the end. You may not need to complete each step and you may need to add a few, depending on your own project (my list assumes you only have one experiment, so you will need to repeat some steps if you have multiple experiments). As when cooking and baking, you may want to read through all of the steps before you begin.

Note, you may need to complete some steps *before* you submit your ethics application, depending on how much detail your ethical approval committee requires. Also note that the sections of the dissertation are not listed in the order your readers will read them, but in the order you will likely write them (see Chapter 5).

Before you officially start (e.g. the spring before)

- Choose a general topic
- Choose a mentor/supervisor
- Meet your mentor (especially important if you were assigned to someone you haven't met!) and discuss his/her expectations for now until you begin
- Begin reading papers on your topic. Ask your mentor for additional relevant papers.

- Submit paperwork for any clearances you will need to work with your population (if applicable).

When you officially start

- Determine your research question (i.e. hypotheses)
- Choose your research design and method (keep your future results section in mind/what results will you obtain?)
- Brainstorm how you will recruit potential participants if there is not a set system in your lab *or* learn the system for recruiting participants or obtaining animals if your mentor already has a system
- Obtain ethical approval (you will need to know your method and design and probably how you will recruit participants as you might need to provide examples of recruitment materials as well)
- Write a procedure (highly recommended)
- Choose your stimuli (if applicable)
- Complete counterbalancing (if applicable)
- Ensure you have access to any equipment you will need and learn how to use it
- Ensure you have access to any software you will need and learn how to use it
- Ensure you know how to reimburse participants (if applicable)
- Decide or learn how you will store any hard data (e.g. forms, if applicable)*
- Decide or learn how you will store any electronic data, including video footage (if applicable)*
- Decide or learn how you will store consent forms*
- Learn computer, phone and photocopier passwords (if applicable)
- If you are testing in a lab make sure you know where everything you will normally need is located
- If you are testing in a lab make sure you know where you are supposed to go in case of a fire or if you need a first-aid kit
- If you are testing off-site make sure you know if there are any additional procedures (e.g. regular check-ins or keeping your student ID with you)
- Continue reading papers on your topic/research question
- Make notes about what to include in your introduction and discussion

*There may already be a set system for your mentor's entire lab. Before you create any system, double-check that a system has not already been predetermined.

Data collection phase

- Print any materials you will need such as questionnaires, consent forms, sheets for which order to present trials in (do not do this until after ethical approval in case the ethics committee requests changes!)
- Recruit a few participants to pilot the procedure
- Pilot the procedure with a few participants/animals, tweak as necessary (be diligent about changing your ethical application if you make changes. Discuss any changes – and ethical application revisions – with your mentor)
- Collect data
- Create files for entering data (if applicable)
- Enter data (if applicable)
- Obtain inter-coder reliabilities (if applicable)
- Measure stimuli (if applicable)
- Take pictures of stimuli (if applicable)
- Write skeleton of participants/subjects paragraph (i.e. without exact numbers)
- Write stimuli/apparatus paragraph
- Write procedure and design section
- Write coding section (if applicable)
- Continue reading papers on your topic/research question
- Continue to make notes about what to include in your introduction and discussion

Post-data collection phase

- Meet with mentor about which statistical analyses you will need and how to do them
- Run statistical analyses (ask questions if you have any!)

Primary writing phase

Methods

- Write or complete participants paragraph
- Write or complete stimuli/apparatus paragraph
- Add a figure about stimuli/apparatus (if applicable)
- Write or complete procedure and design section
- Write or complete coding section (if applicable)
- Send draft(s) of methods section to mentor for comments (if allowed)

Results

- Write paragraph on preliminary analyses (things you don't want to be different between conditions, e.g. age)
- Write results to the hypotheses – add an explanation in plain English after each analysis to tell the reader what the numbers mean in terms of your hypotheses
- Create tables
- Create table captions
- Create figures (format, add error bars, indicators of p-values, etc., as applicable)
- Create figure captions
- Send draft(s) of results section to mentor for comments (if allowed)

Introduction

- Write first paragraph (big picture into the issue)
- Write body of the intro
  - what we already know about the topic
  - questions unanswered in the current literature
  - issues from other studies
- Write ending of the intro (why this particular experiment and what you hope to find/hypotheses)
- Send draft(s) of introduction to mentor for comments (if allowed)

Discussion

- Write first paragraph (summary of what you found; relate to *last* paragraph of the intro)
- Write body of the discussion
  - what these findings tell us that other studies didn't/how they answered unanswered questions or improved other studies
  - limitations (only if there are any)
  - implications
  - directions for future research
- Write last paragraph (why this is the best study ever; relate to big picture in *first* paragraph of the intro)
- Send draft(s) of discussion to mentor for comments (if allowed)

Final steps

- Write abstract
- Write acknowledgements section
- Create references list

- Create title
- Create running head
- Add page numbers

Polishing

- Read through methods and results (including figures and tables) together to make sure you are using the same names for things (e.g. "cake baking condition" versus "cake condition"). Also make sure the figure numbers are correct in the text and the figures (e.g. Figure 1 is labeled Figure 1 and no numbers repeat)
- Find " " and replace with " " (2 spaces → 1 space)
- Take a few days off and then read through the whole thing and look for places to cut words or be more concise – even if you are under the word limit this will improve the writing quality (taking a break is critical so you are less emotionally attached to the words)
- Take at least one more day off. Read through the whole thing once more for typos

Turning it in

- Print dissertation
- Bind dissertation (if required)
- Turn it in
- Celebrate!

Presentation

- Create slides
- Brainstorm on your "elevator pitch" (p. 169)
- Practice
- Practice again with new audience
- Brainstorm on possible questions
- Give presentation
- Celebrate!

Recommended readings

APA and BPS project books

Cone, J. D. & Foster, S. L. (2006). *Dissertations and Theses From Start to Finish: Psychology and Related Fields, Second Edition.* Washington, DC: American Psychological Association.

Foreshaw, M. (2013). *Your Undergraduate Psychology Project.* Chichester, UK: British Psychological Society and John Wiley & Sons Ltd.

Experimental design and projects

Field, A. & Hole, G. (2003). *How to Design and Report Experiments*. London: SAGE Publications.

Harris, P. (2001). *Designing and Reporting Experiments in Psychology, Second Edition*. Maidenhead, UK: Open University Press.

Wood, C., Giles, D. & Percy, C. (2012). *Your Psychology Project Handbook, Second Edition*. London: Pearson.

Writing

Griffies, S. M., Perrie, W. A. & Hull, G. (2013). Elements of Style for Writing Scientific Journal Articles, *Publishing Connect*, (pp. 1–7): Elsevier.

King, S. (2000). *On Writing: A Memoir of the Craft*. New York: Simon & Schuster.

Strunk, W. & White, E. B. (1999). *The Elements of Style, Fourth Edition*. New York: Longman.

Statistics

Morgan, Leech, Gloeckner & Barrett (2012). *IBM SPSS for introductory statistics: Use and interpretation* (5th ed.). Washington, DC: American Psychological Association.

Time management/organization

Allen, D. (2001). *Getting Things Done: How to Achieve Stress-free Productivity*. London: Penguin Books.

Covey, S. R. (1989). *The 7 Habits of Highly Effective People*. New York: Simon & Schuster.

Covey, S. R. & Merrill, A. R. (1994). *First Things First: Coping with the Ever-Increasing Demands of the Workplace*. New York: Simon & Schuster.

Gawande, A. (2011). *The Checklist Manifesto: How to Get Things Right*. London: Profile Books, Ltd.

Vanderkam, L. (2011). *168 Hours: You Have More Time Than You Think*. New York: Portfolio.

References

Allen, D. (2001). *Getting Things Done: How to Achieve Stress-free Productivity*. London: Penguin Books.

Bettmann, M. (2009). Choosing a Research Project and a Research Mentor. *Circulation, 119*, 1832–35. doi: 10.1161/CIRCULATIONAHA.107.752683.

Cone, J. D., & Foster, S. L. (2006). *Dissertations and Theses From Start to Finish: Psychology and Related Fields, Second Edition*. Washington, DC: American Psychological Association.

Covey, S. R. (1989). *The 7 Habits of Highly Effective People*. New York: Simon & Schuster.

Covey, S. R., & Merrill, A. R. (1994). *First Things First: Coping with the Ever-Increasing Demands of the Workplace*. New York: Simon & Schuster.

Field, A., & Hole, G. (2003). *How to Design and Report Experiments*. London: SAGE Publications.

Foreshaw, M. (2013). *Your Undergraduate Psychology Project*. Chichester, UK: British Psychological Society and John Wiley & Sons Ltd.

Fowler, H. N. (1995). *Plato I: Euthyphro, Apology, Crito, Phaedo, Phaedrus*. Cambridge, MA: Harvard University Press.

Gawande, A. (2011). *The Checklist Manifesto: How to Get Things Right*. London: Profile Books, Ltd.

Greenhoot, A. F., & Dowsett, C. J. (2012). Secondary data analysis: An important tool for addressing developmental questions. *Journal of Cognition and Development, 13*(1), 2–18. doi: 10.1080/15248372.2012.646613.

Griffies, S. M., Perrie, W. A., & Hull, G. (2013). Elements of Style for Writing Scientific Journal Articles, *Publishing Connect*, (pp. 1–7): Elsevier.

Harris, P. (2001). *Designing and Reporting Experiments in Psychology, Second Edition*. Maidenhead, UK: Open University Press.

King, S. (2000). *On Writing: A Memoir of the Craft*. New York: Simon & Schuster.

Morgan, G. A., Leech, N. L., Gloeckner, G. W., & Barrett, K. C. (2012). *IBM SPSS for introductory statistics: Use and interpretation* (5th ed.). Washington, DC: American Psychological Association.

Strunk Jr., W., & White, E. B. (1999). *The Elements of Style, Fourth Edition*. New York: Longman.

Vanderkam, L. (2011). *168 Hours: You Have More Time Than You Think*. New York: Portfolio.

Wood, C., Giles, D., & Percy, C. (2012). *Your Psychology Project Handbook, Second Edition*. London: Pearson.

2 All in a day's work

Although "working in the lab" and "collecting data" each sound like one big task, they are both made up of many smaller tasks. Usefully, a lot of the skills you will learn completing these tasks can be used after you graduate because many of these skills are administrative and transferable. Of course, if you use ePrime to test adult participants, it is unlikely that you will use ePrime again. However, you may use the skills you are employing day in and day out when you run your study, e.g., greeting participants, explaining technical details, filing paperwork, answering questions. My goal for this chapter is to help you identify how you can make the most of these skill-acquiring opportunities and also help you to do each of these common daily tasks most effectively.

Creating a "paper trail" or lab notebook

When you start doing research, you are likely to be only working on one study and hopefully that one study will be really important to you. It might feel like you will always remember every detail, every aspect perfectly, just like that perfect date you had that one time. But when you're doing research time flies. Fast. And studies also evolve. In the beginning you may set out to only include data from right-handed participants but then realize that for some reason the study will never be complete, so you need to relax that rule. But maybe suddenly there is a flurry of right-handers and you can go back. But wait, why did you only want right-handers again? Why is that supposed to matter?

In the other sciences, it is very common to create a lab notebook: a place where you can write down things like your study design, critical references, thoughts on those references, etc., and also keep a journal or log of your study as it progresses and evolves. It allows you to go back and read your rationale for various decisions, like why you only wanted to include right-handed participants. Having all of this information in one place can be invaluable when you start to write your method section (or when another lab member starts planning a follow-up experiment).

Your one study is also likely to be only one of a handful of studies your faculty mentor is involved with. Having a lab notebook, or study journal, will allow you to keep a record that *both of you* can go back to later. It is not uncommon for supervisors and mentors to forget method-ological details of studies – especially when they are involved in several studies with similar methods. If you're in a meeting and asked, "Remind me again, what was the delay between trials?" or "Why did we take that item out of the questionnaire?" your study journal may allow you to flip through and provide an answer, even if it boils down to, "You told me to do so in our last meeting."

"In spare time you could make notes for your introduction or discussion. Students seem to randomly think of ideas for future research/limitations/implications but find it hard to remember them when the time comes to write it up."

—Kerri, BSc
Mental Health Recovery Worker

I still use a variation of the lab notebook or study journal today – years after my first study (but see p. 89). Here is a list of some of things I put into my notebooks/journals:

- Criteria for passing training or exclusion and references to other studies that set the precedent.
- What column abbreviations mean in my data files. Example: I know "acc adj" is "accuracy adjusted," but that doesn't tell me how I adjusted it or why.
- Stimuli: number, names, sizes/dimensions, where they were pur-chased and what the product was called. Example: I have used an object I refer to in the journal articles as "rubber pom-pom," but when I bought the first one it was called "worm ball."
- Brief notes on other studies with similar methods to use as examples of how to later write my own method section.
- Notes on figures and tables I found in (other) journal articles that I think would work well in the write-up of the current study. Tip: note the reference and the table number or page number to save time later.
- Notes on what makes this study "better" than related studies (e.g. unique selling points, how it avoids a confound that may be present in another study, tackles an unaddressed issue).

Given that there are several subfields in psychology, your research may not require exactly all of this information and may require other information not listed. Hopefully, this list will give you an idea of the types of information you will want to record before you find yourself saying, "I wish I had written that down somewhere" – or the equally frustrating, "*Where* did I write that down?"

Finding references

General searching

Although Google Scholar is very easy to use and doesn't require a university log in, PsycINFO remains the quintessential tool for searching through the psychology literature (PubMed, Web of Science/Web of Knowledge are good too). PsycINFO allows you to combine and exclude search terms as well as filter by age or only show results that are published articles. This can be problematic with a tool like Google Scholar, which will also give you unpublished articles from personal or lab websites and conference abstracts for talks or posters that you cannot access. I do believe Google Scholar is helpful and sometimes vital (see below), but for the initial searching, it's worth it to get to know PsycINFO. Fortunately, the skills you hone by using PsycINFO can be applied later to other databases like Google Scholar and databases you might use after graduation.

"It is so easy to get side tracked and just read and read different articles all day – but not really achieve much. It is important to list articles and come back to them. Keep a separate file/list/folder on your computer of articles to come back to along with a note of where you suspect they could fit into your paper.

"If you can, update your reference list. (Do this daily as you go along! Otherwise you have a nightmare at the end, when you are feeling most stressed, with the deadline fast approaching!)"

—Sam, BSc
Life Skills Recovery Worker, NHS

There are a few different ways to go about searching for literature relevant to your topic. The first is to take a broad keyword and search for that keyword. But that approach will likely give you far more papers than you can ever read and many papers that will be too far removed from your aspect of that topic. For example, I've just searched for "sleep," and the ten most recently published papers that came up included several about the cognitive deficits of too little sleep (including one in Parkinson's disease), two about child sleep, one about employees' work engagement and another about US military personnel. If your project were on studying habits and sleep, few, if any, of these papers would be relevant. Even if your paper were on cognitive deficits and sleep, several of these papers would be irrelevant. This is why filters can be so critical.

You can use the software to filter results, e.g. showing only journal articles, only about "REM sleep" and only with adult participants and only written in English. That will decrease the number of articles to sift through.

Alternatively, you can add additional keywords under the "advanced" tab. For example, in the realm of sleep research, if I search for *sleep* and *student* or *study* I'm given almost 20,000 fewer papers to look through. I could refine even more by also applying filters like those above. When using keywords, take advantage of the lines where you can specify ___ or ___. It is often helpful to use synonyms or related words there (e.g. student or study, child or children, rat or animal model). You can also add additional lines to include other keywords. If you want keywords to always appear together, you can search for them in quotes (e.g. "infant sleep"). Finally, instead of combining keywords, you can select "not" instead of "and." That will allow you to search something like *sleep* not *child* or *children*. Fortunately, most topics aren't as popular as sleep, so you will not have to deal with so many papers.

Another great starting point is asking your supervisor for some names of key authors (or look at the references of his or her papers). When I was a student sometimes my mentors would give me names but only give me surnames (last names). This would drive me nuts! If you only search for someone by surname, you're apt to get records for several people from a variety of sub-disciplines. I was too shy to admit that I had no idea who they meant, so I rarely asked for the first names. At other times I've been interested in reading a paper noted in a reference list and only have initials and a last name. If you do Google a last name and the topic or surname and "psychology" you can often find the website of the person who was recommended to you. You may still find a few people with similar names, but you can usually quickly see from their research interests who it is that you want.

What to do when you don't have access

Journal publishers make money through subscriptions and charging for individual articles, copies and copyright fees. Most universities subscribe to several journals and some publishers own several journals that they bundle together. But sometimes a particular journal is not included in a bundle or is not owned by a major publisher (this does not necessarily mean it is not a good journal!). So, you might someday find that you would like to read something that you cannot access through your university website.

Many universities have interlibrary loan services, which allow them to share materials with another library, for example a nearby university's library. Ask your library (or look for this on your library's website) to find out more. You often have to complete a request form with a lot of information about the item you are requesting (volume, issue, starting page number, authors' names, etc.). Some universities charge a small fee for requests, and each request can take several days to complete (sometimes you will receive a hardcopy instead of a PDF).

If interlibrary loan does not sound like a solution for you, then here are some other methods to track down the paper in the order I recommend you try them:

1. Ask your mentor (and then other lab members) if he or she has a copy. Others may have already been through this hassle.
2. Google the article title. That may bring you to the journal website where you can download the article if it is "open access" (which means the authors used funds from the organization that funded the research to pay the costs for the paper so you don't need a subscription to access the article). It may also bring you to another page that has a copy (e.g. one of the authors' websites). You may need to put quotation marks around the title depending on the popularity of the words in the title.
3. Google the first author and/or last authors to see if they have a copy on their websites. Often these versions will be the double-spaced manuscript version, but the text should be identical to the typeset, published version.
4. Email the "corresponding author." The information you have about the paper from the journal website or PsycINFO should indicate the corresponding author and include an email address. If your email does not go through, look up the author; he or she may have moved

to a new university (or you may need to try another author). Be sure to introduce yourself in your email and be clear about which paper you would like to read because "your 2015 paper on [topic]" or "your Psych Science paper" might not be enough if the author has several papers on that topic from that year or in that journal.

Forward searching

One way to find related references is to look through the reference list at the end of the article you are reading. An additional highly useful way to do a literature search is to do a cited reference search (a.k.a. a forward search). When you look up an article, there will usually be text underneath that says something like "cited by" and a number. If you click on that it will give you a list of papers that have since cited the original paper that you are looking at. This new list of papers should include any study that replicated the original study (or found a flaw with it) or used the original study and its implications for a new line of research or to answer related questions. So, a lot of the papers on that list should be highly relevant to you. Of course, sometimes people fail to cite relevant literature, so relying exclusively on this list is not going to be enough for your literature search. Also, some authors will only cite a paper tangentially to make a very minor point, so not every paper on the list may be relevant. Overall, though, this kind of search is a really useful place to start.

Each literature search engine (e.g. PsycINFO, Google Scholar, Web of Science) gets its information from different sources than the others, so the "cited by" lists will be slightly different within each search engine. They will overlap, but no list will have every paper that cited the original article (so you might want to look in multiple places). Also, in Web of Science you can do a two-generation cited reference search to also view the papers that cited the papers that cited the original paper.

Many literature search engines will also send you alerts if a new paper enters the system (usually within a couple of months of being published) that cites a given paper or uses a certain keyword. Look for a button that says "citation alert" or "email alert" to sign yourself up to be alerted.

A good many journal articles (organization)

Relative to the other sciences, psychology is a young science, but you'd hardly ever guess that based on the number of journal articles you can find on almost any topic. There is a lot to read and a lot to remember. There is also a lot that can be forgotten or hard to find again like a needle in a stack of needles (Spielberg, 1998).

Organizing journal articles

Over time I've tried a few different ways of organizing journal articles (both PDFs and hardcopies), and the method that seems to work the best is sorting them alphabetically by first author's last name (surname). Sometimes I sort an article by corresponding author (usually this is the last author), if I know it is like another article from that same lab.

Of course, the whole point of keeping and storing the article is so you can go back to it later. So, this method will only work if you remember the authors' names! I have actually met the vast majority of the authors whose articles I have in my filing cabinet and on my computer, but when I am starting to read up on a new research topic a lot of the names don't "mean" anything to me. This probably sounds familiar. What to do?

If you read hard copies, it can be really useful to write notes on the top of a paper that can jog your memory. For example, you might write "kids don't remember words after five minutes" on Horst and Samuelson (2008). Then, if you forget the authors' names you can at least flip through your papers and look for your note.

If you only read papers as PDFs, it is more effective to save keywords as part of the file name so you can search your computer for the file (e.g. Horst_Samuelson_2008-forget-words-5-minutes). Sometimes I still name files like this and eventually once I have memorized the reference I change the name of the file. If you take this approach, be careful to use the keywords you think you would search for (e.g. are you more likely to think of "remember" or "forget"?), or if you still can't find a file, try searching for a related keyword. (Note, strategic file naming and notes on hardcopies are not mutually exclusive!)

As soon as you can, do yourself a favor and try to get in the habit of referring to the papers you read by their references. "The one where kids don't remember words after five minutes" is OK when you are brainstorming about your introduction, but that's not how you are going to cite it, so eventually you will want to know the reference.

"I made a PowerPoint early on and added any information/idea/ papers I found as I went along and thought would be useful; that way I had it all in one place. Then when I started writing I had a lot of information to work from."

—Kerri, BSc
Mental Health Recovery Worker

Keeping track of all the findings

As you read more and more papers, it can be difficult to keep the findings straight. Because scientific research is methodical, many papers will build on each other, use similar methods and make controlled changes from a previous paper. In other words: there is a lot that can seem the same.

One useful way to keep track of things is to use a notes app (e.g. Evernote, GoogleKeep, Trello) where you can store images and text. For example, you can save your own sketch of the method in a study you want to cite.

Another useful lower-tech way to keep track of several studies that are similar in some ways is by making a table. I highly recommend making a table in Word, Excel or a similar program because you can use the computer to search for a keyword or phrase (e.g. "five minutes") so you don't have to re-read your whole table every time you want to look something up. Plus you can make a back-up. See Table 2.1 for an example of a few rows from one of my tables.

Making a table like that can help you filter through the relevant information and keep you from getting bogged down by the details. You may discover later that such tables are useful for other information as well, such as information about specific clients.

TABLE 2.1
Example of a table for keeping track of studies

Word Learning Studies

Study	Age(s)	Task	Delay
Hollich et al., 2000	24 mos	Preferential looking, items displayed on both monitors during naming and test	1 wk *unsuccessful*
Markson & Bloom, 1997	3–4 yrs	Measure objects	None, 1 wk, 1 mo, *successful*
Mervis & Bertrand, 1994: Expt. 1.	16–20 mos	Fast mapping; 5-alt. forced choice	2 trials later, *only post-vocab-spurt kids successful*
Mervis & Bertrand, 1994: Expt. 2.	16–20 mos: *retested low vocab kids after spurt*	Fast mapping; 5-alt. forced-choice	2 trials later, *successful*

Box 2.1: Storing articles

Sometimes it is worth it to have a few smaller folders with papers on very specific topics. For example, in my filing cabinet I have a folder called "missing data" that includes papers on how to handle missing data points in statistical analyses. Because I only dip into these papers rarely (hopefully never again!), it's easier to sort these by topic.

Many students sort *all* of their papers by topic. I did it that way when I first started out in psychology too, but I quickly discovered that this can be problematic because some papers are on multiple topics. For example, a paper on learning names for categories could belong with other language papers or other categorization papers.

As mentioned in the main text, I generally sort articles alphabetically by the first author's last name (or sometimes by the "senior author," the head of the lab that conducted the research. Often this is the last author). Once someone has a few papers in my pile, he or she gets a folder, which makes it easier for me to find his/her papers later. I don't think it is very economic to create a folder when I only have one paper by someone; papers like this are filed by letter. For example, at any given time I might have seven papers in my "W" folder.

On my computer I do the same thing: I have a folder called "articles" and then within that about twenty-three folders by letter (some letters are combined, e.g. XYZ). On the computer I don't have folders for each author/lab because it is faster to just scroll through the alphabetical list and all of the White papers will be next to each other. I name my electronic files things like *Plum_et_al_2007.pdf* or *Peacock_Green_1999.pdf*. Sometimes if I'm struggling to learn the reference of a new-to-me article, I'll put something in the file name to help me find it (e.g. *Mustard_et_al_2014_Clue-Cluedo_Game.pdf*).

Tip: Binders

I have learned through experience that keeping articles in binders instead of folders can be problematic because they are prone to increased wear and tear, including literally tearing off where the holes are punched. If you are dead set on binders you may want to use page protectors (document wallets) as well.

Finding participants

Fliers

If you need to recruit participants through something besides a departmental online sign-up system, it can be useful to make fliers where people can tear off the name of your study and your contact info. Do include your contact information on the main part of the flier in case the last tab is torn off and someone wants the info (periodically check if your fliers need replacing). Hang fliers in locations where your potential participants are likely to go (e.g. bulletin boards in grocery stores, near restrooms on campus). Often you need permission to use bulletin boards, so follow any requirements like that.

Canvassing individuals

Depending on your target population you may want to canvas individuals. When people meet a real person, it makes the research less abstract and daunting. It also allows the potential participants to ask questions. If you are literally planning to hand out fliers in a very public place, for example at the entrance to a shopping center, you may need to obtain permission first. Do not skip this step!

Another approach is to look through online event calendars and magazines that your target population might look through and identify locations where you might try to recruit. Most of my students' projects involve testing children so we keep a list of local childcare facilities and places that offer classes like baby yoga, where we might find parents and children. Next, we contact the service provider (e.g. childcare center or baby yoga class) and ask if we can come at the end of the sessions to tell parents about the lab and what we do. Be sure to approach parents at the *end* of the session, not at the start: though they may be dashing off, you do not want to intrude on time they are paying for.

In my lab we keep records of who we contacted, how helpful they were, who we spoke to and who from the lab went to meet parents. This helps us avoid asking the same service provider if we can visit too frequently, which isn't just annoying for them but also not so productive for us because it can take several months before new members join the group and we will already have met the current members. However, you may wish to go to different sessions to catch different people (e.g. the Tuesday class and Wednesday class).

It is also polite to offer to reciprocate the service provider in some way, such as putting one of their posters or fliers up in your lab waiting room or communicating your research findings to them after your study is complete (without identifying any of the participants, of course). You and your lab may also be able to "like" or "follow" them on social media.

When you show up to canvas, bring your university ID card to prove you are legit and who you say you are. Make joining your mailing list as easy on the potential participants as possible: instead of (or in addition to) a flier that directs them to a website, ask for the most minimal information you need now so they don't have to do anything.

> "I am now delivering an anger management program; and as in the lab where we would increase awareness in the community about the lab, I do the same here, spreading the word, creating flyers and contacting prison officers and offender supervisors and educating them about the course first to see if they would recommend any prisoners to attend."
>
> —Kirsten, MSc
> Assistant Psychologist, Prison Service

Snowballing

Snowballing is also an effective means of recruiting from some populations. Like how one snowflake will attach to several new snowflakes as a snowball rolls down a hill, in this method one participant will recommend one or more additional participants. Basically, do you have any friends or know anyone else who might want to do this study?

The advantage of snowballing is that your participants can do some of the work for you, which can be especially difficult if you need to recruit from a highly specialized sample (e.g. individuals who have spent time in prison, bilingual children, former expats). But you will likely want to use other recruitment methods as well so that you can complete your data collection on time (read: don't rely solely on snowballing). Also keep in mind that your first participants could have a bigger impact on your study because they will have had longer to recommend new participants and your sample may not be quite as random as you would want in theory – but psychology participants are pretty "weird" anyway (Henrich, Heine, & Norenzayan, 2010).

Team up

Depending on the nature of your study, someone else in your department might be running a study with a similar population but investigating something completely different that will have little chance of influencing your results. For example, if you are testing 7-year-olds and adults in a digit-span task and someone else is testing 7-year-olds and adults in a face-recognition task, you may be able to team up and tell your participants about each other's study at the end of their experiments – or if the experiments are short enough, schedule both sessions for the same day so the participant only has to travel once. Do not make this decision alone, however: run it by both of your supervisors to ensure there isn't some weird effect that could contaminate your data if participants take part in both studies. To increase the chances that you reach your target sample size, do not rely on this method to gain additional participants, but if you do get another participant, think of it as a bonus.

How to write an email that gets answered

Learning how to effectively communicate via email may be one of the most valuable transferable skills you learn during your research. As businesses become more "global," email is continuing to be very important, especially as people increase their need to communicate with others in different time zones. When working in the lab, you will likely send many emails to your mentor and others. Both the number of emails you receive and the speed with which they arrive may surprise you. You may even send emails to recruit participants.

I want to help you write emails that are professional, but perhaps more importantly, I want to help you write emails that actually get answered in a reasonable timeframe.

"Perhaps the most important skills I developed were communication skills. The constant emails seemed excessive to me at first, but after several weeks in the lab I learned how critical it was that everyone was informed. Not only could new people easily be brought up to speed on a current project, but the paper trail also allowed us to juggle multiple deadlines and collaborate with other labs on different continents with minimal hassles."

—Marena, BSc
PhD student

Make it easy

The "secret" to writing an email that gets answered quickly is to make replying as easy as possible for the recipient.

First have an informative subject line, especially if your email has information the recipient might want to look at again in the future. Think about the emails you receive. Isn't it easier to find the date when you can expect a package when there is one email with words like "order confirmation" or "receipt" in the subject line and another email with words like "item dispatched" in the subject line? How obnoxious would it be if you had dozens of emails with subject lines like "online shopping update"?

> "Most correspondence is done with email, so I think it's handy to know what to say, how to say it . . ."
>
> —Matt, BSc
> PhD student

Before you write your email, ask yourself what the "action points" are. What do you want to get out of the email? Are you simply sending information, or do you have a request, an "action" that you need the reader to take?

If you are simply sending an update or information, make the email as easy as possible for the recipient by providing all of the necessary information in the first email so he or she doesn't have to ask follow-up questions. For example, "[the computer software] crashed again when I tried to test a participant" might lead to follow-up questions that could be avoided by writing "[the computer software] crashed again when I tried to test a participant. I was running [condition] and the screen went blue right after I entered the participant's date of birth and hit return." (Note, if you are in a situation where data might be lost or equipment is not working, the phone may be a better choice than email!)

If you need an answer or more information, make the email as easy as possible for the recipient by avoiding open-ended questions whenever possible. Instead, try to use yes/no questions or questions where the answer could be "the first one" or "the second thing you said." For example, "What should I do with the participants scheduled for tomorrow?" will require a lengthy reply. If the recipient doesn't have a lot of time when your email comes it could take a long time to write that lengthy reply. In contrast, "Should I just test participants in Condition B or should I reschedule everyone until we get this sorted?" can be answered quickly ("Yes, test in B for now" or "Reschedule. I'll come to the lab after my next meeting.").

Another reason why it is useful to avoid open-ended questions or no constraints on options is because it can make it harder for you to reply back. Imagine you are sending emails to invite people to be in your study. Hopefully, you will get many responses and some people might even write back with their availability (e.g. "I can do your study on Friday!"). If you already know when you are sending the email that you can never run the study on Friday (class, work, someone else in the lab using the equipment that day, etc.), you can save yourself work by noting something like, "This study can take place at a time to suit your schedule Mondays through Thursdays." (For more information on using email to recruit participants, see p. 39.)

Make it short

Don't go on and on. For example, in the email, "I have been testing participants this week. So far I have tested ten participants (eight females, two males)," the first seven words do not provide any substantial content that the second sentence doesn't cover. Emails should be shorter than letters but longer than text messages. Two paragraphs seems about average.

One caveat: some supervisors prefer to get more, smaller units of information in their emails and others prefer fewer emails. Try to determine the style your supervisor prefers (you can even ask). If your supervisor prefers that you put all of your questions into a single email, do that, but still keep your email brief and each point easy to "action."

Make it legit

If you are using email to recruit participants, use your university email or your lab's email address. Not everyone has an .edu or .ac.uk email address, but anyone could pretend to be a researcher using a Hotmail or similar email account.

Finally, another way to speed up recipient responses when you are emailing someone within your university (but not the lab group) is to copy your faculty mentor in, especially if you are emailing that person for the first time. For example, imagine you need to email an administrator in your department to request special visitor parking passes for your study. The administrator may see your email and have questions such as: who is this person? Does this person really work in that lab? Who is paying for the parking passes? When you copy in your faculty mentor, the administrator will see that this is a legitimate request, ask any follow-up questions (e.g. payment) and can act on it faster. I have seen a lot of requests delayed simply because the recipient had to check the request was from a legitimate lab member!

This final tip is also helpful because there may be other things going on now or previously of which you are not aware. For example, another student may have made a similar request and now there is a question about whether this wasn't already dealt with or if these are two separate requests. Or your mentor could know that a particular administrator will respond faster if the mentor replies with a grant code to charge.

Box 2.2: To the letter: Email dos and don'ts

- Have an informative subject line.
- Address the recipient with "Dear" or at least something more formal than "Hey" or "Hiya."
- If you haven't emailed the person in the last three months, clearly identify yourself (e.g., "I'm a research assistant in ____ lab.").
- Enable spell check in your email software or settings.
- Use the same capitalization and punctuation as you would in a journal article. Also include paragraph breaks (it can be difficult to read large blocks of text via email).
- Be succinct: if your email is more than three paragraphs, it may be too long.
- Provide contact information, especially for people with whom you do not interact frequently. This can be as simple as a telephone number and repeating your email address after your name.
- Consider bolding important information (e.g. your phone number, a specific room or date/time) if it is buried in the middle of the paragraph.
- Number your points if you have a lot of points to cover in a single email.
- Use real words instead of emoticons – at least for recipients with whom you do not interact frequently ;-)
- Use reply-all with caution. Does everyone on the email really need to read your response? Sometimes this is useful, but sometimes it just wastes time.

- Keep in mind that once you hit "send" your email could be forwarded to anyone. If you are writing something you would *not* like someone to read (e.g. a complaint about another lab member), use the phone or speak in person.
- Sign your name.

Mail merge: among the most useful transferable skills

When I started brainstorming about this book, I asked several of my previous students about the skills that they learned by doing their research that they then used after graduation when they started their jobs. At least half of the students raved about how useful it has been to know how to do "mail merge" even though many had never heard of it before they started in the lab.

> "Learning how to mail merge from when we were contacting participants was a fantastic skill which I have used to save mammoth amounts of time in all of the jobs I have had since graduating."
> —Rosa, BSc
> Senior Program Manager (Charity Sector)

Mail merge is a feature in Word that allows you to take a document (like a letter or email) and send it to multiple people *with information specific to them* instead of general information. You have likely received letters/emails generated using mail merge, but they often appear very personal. For example, you may have received an email addressed to you (Dear [your name]) with information relevant to you (e.g. "You are currently registered for the following classes: . . .") rather than generic information (e.g. "to see which modules you are registered for, log into . . .").

Mail merge can be extremely helpful if you would like to email several potential participants but have each email individually addressed. In my lab we frequently use mail merge to email families with children in a certain age range and are able to set up the emails so they sound fairly personal, e.g., "Dear Jessica, I'm emailing to invite James to participate in a new study . . ."

Mail merge is among the "tools" in Word. I had heard of it but taught myself how to use it by looking it up online and then first trying it out with a couple of my own email addresses. First, you create an Excel file with the individual information. For example, you might have one column with First Name and another with Email Address. Second, following the instructions from Word, you tell Word which Excel file has the relevant information. Next, you write your letter or email as you normally would, but everywhere where you would write information that you want to be specific (e.g. "Dear [Individual]"), you drag-and-drop the column name that you used for that information in Excel (e.g. First Name). When you are finished you can preview the letters/emails and then either print them or send them to Outlook, where they will be sent as regular emails.

If you have a lot of people to email, this is also helpful because if anyone replies you will see what you wrote them (e.g. scrolling down we can see the child's name) and no one can "reply-all." Not to mention that each email can look like it was individually written, which can be useful for making recipients feel that they have your individual attention (useful for sales, and other industries, because customers enjoy feeling treated like individuals).

A few tips: do not change the font colors for the information you are adding (it could be quite embarrassing if each time you use a certain name it was always in a different color to the rest of the email!). Also, I try to write my original text in such a way that it would still sound OK if I were to forget one of the places where I meant to drag-and-drop individual information. So, for example, I might write "We hope to see you and your child soon!" instead of "We hope to see you and child's name soon!"

> "Also having templates of emails (which can be altered) was really useful just to be confident in your communication."
>
> —Ruth, BSc
> Family Support Practitioner (Charity Sector)

Contacting participants by phone

If you are fortunate enough to be recruiting and testing typical undergraduates, you very likely will be able to use some kind of online sign-up system that will automatically remind both your participants and you when your sessions are and enable participants to cancel (and inform you). Many of the rest of us need to recruit participants by phone.

"In particular, my ability to approach parents, strike up a conversation about the research I was conducting and convince them to participate in the study built up my confidence in my current role where I am placed in a position to sell a service to the general public and approach people to inform them about a product and convince them to sign up. This is a skill I have used every day of my working life."

—Naureen, BSc
Education Center Manager

When you call, introduce yourself early. Try to get a sense of which salutations work well in your area. I thought when I moved to the prim and proper UK that starting, "May I speak to Mr. Smith, please?" would work well, but actually, that sounds suspiciously like telemarketing and "This is Jessica from the Word Lab. May I speak with Dave?" is much more successful.

If you are recruiting participants by phone and are not the only researcher working on a given study (e.g. you are part of a team), it is useful to make notes on the participant's record/form about when you called and what the result was (this can also be helpful even if you are the only one recruiting for the study). For example, if you have left a voice message and noted the time and date, ideally with your initials, the next time a team member calls your teammate can help the lab appear very organized by saying something like "Jessica told me she left a voice message for you on Friday. I was wondering if you have considered participating or if I can tell you more about the study." If you are struggling to recruit participants by phone, keeping notes like this will also allow you to check if you have been calling at the same time every day. You may want to mix up the time of day that you call, because they may have a set time for going to the gym or other regularly scheduled activities.

"I realized how important it is to log all contact made with participants and to keep really clear and organized notes in a database so that other colleagues can share the information and there is no repetition."

—Kirsten, MSc
Assistant Psychologist, Prison Service

If you have already sent an email or letter when you get a participant on the phone, ask if she has received that information and if she
would like to hear more. If the response is, "No, I didn't see your email"
rather than say, "Oh, OK, I'll call back later after you have a chance to
read that," ask if you can tell her about the study "since we are already
on the phone." It is *much easier* to talk to someone you already have on
the phone than to reach him on the phone again. I cannot stress this
enough. Often it's also easier for participants to hear you talk about a
study and ask questions as they come up or give you cues (e.g. "uh huh,
uh huh") as they are listening that enable you to know to speed up what
you are telling them.

If a participant cannot talk now, politely offer to call back at a time
that is more convenient for them – and make sure you stick to it. Participants are doing you a favor listening to your spiel about your study so
you want to be courteous and respectful of that. I've learned through
(bad) experience that if a participant says he wants to call you back, it
is very helpful to include a statement such as, "If I don't hear back from
you by next Friday, may I call back then?" That allows the participant
to save face if he forgets to ring you back and also allows you to warmly
start the next conversation with, "We agreed I'd call/ring you back on
Friday" rather than, "I didn't hear back from you" (read: you didn't keep
your commitment/you lied).

Box 2.3: Be careful what you say (describing studies)

When you go over your consent form, you should be very precise
and honest when describing the task so your participants can really
provide informed consent, accurately know what to expect and identify any questions they want to ask. However, when describing your
study during the recruiting phase, your potential participants only
need a general idea of the task to decide if they want to schedule
sessions. To be clear, I am *not* recommending that you deceive your
participants about what your study is about or what your task is like.
Just think carefully about how much information to provide because
you do not want to give participants so much information that they
can practice the study and therefore compromise your results.

In my lab we often conduct word learning studies in which children are given three objects at a time (left, middle, right) and are
asked for each one in turn. Typically, when I recruit for such studies I
might explain, "We'll give your child some objects like a toy car and a

whisk and ask for a 'blicket.' If he knows the car is a car, he should use the process of elimination to pick the other thing." One student, however, was much more specific. This student scheduled a child who came into the lab and only chose objects in the middle. Upon leaving the lab, the parent remarked, "Hmm, I wonder if she only ever picked the thing in the middle because that's where I always put the one I wanted her to get when I practiced with her at home yesterday." And poof! At least an hour of time was unnecessarily wasted (not to mention the expense).

When you have your participants on the phone and they have agreed to schedule a session, make sure you get any prescreen information before they hang up. If your participants need to be right-handed, have 20/20 vision or not be bilingual it is much easier to get this information on the phone now than to try to reach them sometime in the future.

Also, if your participant fails to meet some of the criteria (e.g. a left-handed, legally blind bilingual individual), it is much easier to say, "Oh, actually, for this particular study we can only recruit. . . ." And let them down gently rather than waste any more of their time and yours.

Keep in mind that you may need to ask questions beyond prescreening – for example if they are coming by car or public transportation, if other children are coming, if they need directions.

At the end of your phone call, give participants a number to reach you on (if they need to reschedule). If you are comfortable and allowed to give them your phone number please do that – it will be much faster to reach you, especially if the session is the first one of the day! Also reconfirm the date, day of the week and time (e.g. "OK, we'll see you on Thursday the 12th at 10:00.").

You will also want to confirm the appointment the day before to ensure they are still planning to show up. This is especially important if you schedule more than one week in advance because plans change and things come up. It is much easier to reschedule an appointment before they are due to participate than to get them to reschedule after they have failed to show up when not showing up is now the default. On occasion when the weather has been particularly bad (e.g. heavy snow), I have also re-confirmed the morning of the appointment and offered to reschedule because I want my participants to be happy and enjoy their experience in the lab so that they are willing to participate in future studies.

"My project enabled me to call and communicate with parents to invite their child to participate. I learnt good communication skills that I have transferred into my teaching job where I talk to difficult parents daily."

—Lauren L. BSc
Teacher

When you are recruiting participants, you want to pay attention to how many participants you actually need. Despite your best efforts, some people will fail to show up and some people will fail to provide viable data (e.g. children cry, undergraduates just go through the motions, fire alarms go off). For this reason, I try to schedule a couple of participants more than I think I will need, only about one or two additional male and female participants. Then, I keep an eye on how close I am to completing data collection. You do not want to be in a situation where you only need one more male participant but have seven scheduled! However, if your study is one of a series of related studies, then it may be possible for the additional participants to take part in the next experiment in the series.

Never mention to a participant that his/her data is "extra" because you may later discover that you need to exclude the data for another participant and this is now very real, important data (e.g. if you discover during your analyses that you have to replace an outlier). Also, you do not want to give the impression that you are wasting participants' time because word will spread and people will not want to do studies in your lab anymore.

Box 2.4: Common sense

When you are recruiting and testing participants, use common sense. On some level you are representing your department, your university and psychologists in general. Participants see you as a professional researcher, so act that way (wear suitable clothes, do not take personal calls, keep your phone on silent and don't use profanity or offensive language, even if it seems like something small or a way to start getting a rapport going, e.g. "yeah, that damn parking ticket machine always gets stuck").

Stimuli

If your study involves physical objects (tangrams, novel objects, the Tower of Hanoi, etc.) record in your lab notebook (p. 24) the stimulus dimensions and where you purchased your stimuli (and the product name) in case you need to find a replacement quickly or someone else in your lab group wants another one sometime later. When working with children I try to order multiples of items before I start a study in case something breaks (toddlers love throwing and banging things). I have learned the hard way that this is also helpful because toy manufacturers "improve" products frequently, for example, by adding LED lights or changing the color, so it is not always possible to find an identical replacement.

"If you need to buy stimuli, get them as soon as you know what you need. It may take a while to find what you are looking for."
—Matt, BSc
PhD Student

Photographing stimuli and apparatuses

If the stimuli for your research includes equipment or physical objects, it may be helpful to include a figure (photograph) in your paper. This may be especially important if anyone reading your project is from a different research area (and therefore may be less familiar with this kind of stimuli or equipment). Photographs of equipment are more striking with a person in the photo, and it might be worth trying to take the photograph from several angles to choose the best one later. "Action shots" like this are also sometimes helpful for lab or project websites if you want to give readers an idea of the kind of research you do. Such photography skills can be used later if you need to take photos for product sales or company promotional materials.

If you are photographing physical objects, take the photographs as early on in the data-collection phase as possible before anything becomes dirty, worn out or broken. Once, several months after I finished running a study, I went back to photograph all of the balls and blocks the toddlers had played with in the study – only to find that a big chunk was missing from one of the foam balls! To create a photograph that depicted the stimuli as the children had seen them, I had to stuff the ball with tissue paper until it looked round again – fortunately no one can see in the photograph that the back side is completely exposed! In another study, the final toddler participant took a big bite out of a similar ball!

When I take photographs of physical objects I lay a large piece of white paper on a table (or tape it to a wall and then let it drape over a table) as a backdrop. Some objects are fiddly, so I sometimes use tiny amounts of tape to help the objects stand up or lay flat. Use as much light as possible to avoid shadows. You may find it helpful to stand on a step stool or chair (without wheels!) to take the photo from above. (For a discussion of different types of stimulus figures and related tips see p. 147.)

Measuring stimuli

You may also need to measure your stimuli so that you can include the sizes or weights of the objects, the distance the participant sat from the screen or the visual angle in your method section. It is useful to record these measurements in your lab notebook (p. 24) and to do this during downtime (p. 79).

If you paint your stimuli keep a record of the paint colors you use. This is especially important if you have had to mix colors (e.g., one part black to three parts teal) or choose specific values for various features on a computer (e.g., the cyan, magenta, yellow and key [CMYK] values). If the paint from your stimuli chips off you will be glad to know the exact color to use to touch it up!

Piloting and early stage of data collection

Expect to complete a period of piloting before you begin your "real" data collection – even if you are using a method your supervisor has used numerous times before. Piloting isn't only helpful to get any kinks out of the system so participants can complete the task as you intended, but also so you can practice running the study yourself.

Before you even begin piloting, try to find someone in your lab group who is willing to do a dress rehearsal with you. Ideally you want someone like a PhD student or post-doc (or even your faculty mentor) who has been running similar studies for a long time and has an idea of what could go wrong. Collect all of your paperwork, including the consent form, and then set up your experiment as if you are really running it. Walk your partner through the consent form.

Box 2.5: Sample size

This book is not about experimental design (it's about the logistics of conducting research). Before you begin your study you should discuss your target sample size with your supervisor. If you are unsure where to begin, look for sections about sample size and power in the books from your statistics classes. You may also consider reading one of the experimental design books recommended at the end of chapter 1.

Honestly, this can feel a little awkward or intimidating at first, particularly if you are practicing with a faculty member. You could try practicing with a peer first, but your peer might not notice if you do something wrong, or might only recognize that something is wrong but not know how to make it right. Worst-case scenario your peer could be doing something wrong that you are doing right, but your peer mistakenly tells you the wrong way is the correct way. So, it's much better to get the information from as high up the chain as possible. Just keep in mind that there was once a day when the clever post-doc or your faculty mentor was in your shoes and ran his/her first participant too.

Go through the consent form and then the experimental procedure or interview. When I practice with my students I spend the first while helping the student get the mechanics down by performing well as a participant. Then, I find it helpful to start going through some of the things the student could face – in my lab this means toy throwing, kids just staring at their shoes without responding, ambiguous responses, etc. If your partner is willing, asking him/her to act like a "bad participant" can be helpful so that if you do face a real participant engaging in "bad behavior" you know how to handle it.

In my experience it is not uncommon for more than one thing to go wrong with someone's first participant. For example, if there is an age limit and a training threshold and something the experimenter needs to remember to say, chances are good that at least two of those three things will go wrong in the first session. So, expect your first session might not be very good.

In addition to piloting, you may want to set a milestone (e.g. after four participants) at which point you sit down with your supervisor and check that the study is running properly. Just because participants are finishing doesn't mean the method is correct. If something is going wrong, for example, your participants are taking much longer than someone else's in the same task, you may want to complete another dress rehearsal to troubleshoot what you are doing differently.

Box 2.6: Two pilot study anecdotes

One reason why piloting is so important is because sometimes methods simply do not work. For example, I once tried to replicate and extend a study that included an experimental condition and a control condition. I planned to run a different experimental condition and the same control condition, so I started testing children in the control condition. My control group pilots performed significantly worse than those in the original study. There was no way I was going to replicate that condition, so it was moot to even consider the experimental group. This failure turned out to lead me to investigate some other issues that blossomed into a lucrative line of research, but at the time it was frustrating and almost scary. However, I'm grateful that I first tried the control group instead of beginning with both conditions.

Similarly, sometimes it's not the methods but the stimuli. A friend of mine once conducted an elegant infant categorization study in which all infants saw the same familiarization stimuli, but the order they were presented in varied between conditions. At test infants were exposed to old items and new items. Based on previous studies there should have been a clear advantage for one condition over the other – but my friend found no difference! She went back and ran a discrimination study to ensure that infants at this age could tell the difference between the items and discovered that they could not. If they couldn't tell the difference between the items of course they wouldn't be able to tell what was old and new on the test trials. She ended up running a new discrimination study and a new main experiment, both with a new set of stimuli. Those studies worked – but the process cost her a lot of time and money. If only she had run the preliminary discrimination study first. An engineer would say "measure twice, cut once."

If you are not the only person running an experiment you also want to ensure everyone is following the exact same method. For this reason it can be helpful to write a protocol or procedure with step-by-step instructions. It is difficult to have too much detail in your protocol. Such protocols are also extremely valuable when it is time to write your method section. Creating protocols for you and others is a useful, transferable skill. In your next job you might find that there are tasks you complete regularly but not often (e.g. filing expense claims) for which you want a protocol so that you can refresh yourself on where to click and what number to enter where to save time. Protocols can also be helpful for training other staff and ensuring everyone follows the same procedure when interacting with clients.

You may want to schedule gaps between participants for the first few participants you test so you can get a good sense of how long the study really takes before you start testing as many people as you can in one day.

When you are testing participants, have a contingency plan ready in case the first participant is late/slow and the next one arrives early. Can the next participant complete some paperwork while he or she waits? Can you move the first participant to another desk to wrap up? Participants are always volunteering their time (even if it is in exchange for course credit) so you don't want them to feel like they are wasting their time waiting if the person before them is taking too long. Usually participants know if they are early, but sometimes there are still overlaps. You may want to schedule brief gaps in between sessions to account for this (and to allow yourself to take breaks for email, snacks and the restroom). It will always take participants longer to complete a study they are new to than it will take you to practice/ pretend to do the task.

For some experiments your computer will randomly select each trial for a given participant. For other experiments you will create a set of counterbalanced orders (see Chapter 1) for your participants to complete. If your study involves the latter, cycle through all of the orders before you repeat. For example, if your second participant was tested in Order 7A but didn't pass the training criterion, wait until you have used all of the other orders until you give Order 7A to another participant. Why? Because sometimes researchers change their minds and an excluded participant is welcomed back into the real sample. For example, a new paper could come out demonstrating that a different training criterion is just as good and suddenly you could be three participants closer to completing your data collection if you used the new criterion.

Testing off campus

Most of my advice is coming from testing in a lab located on campus, because that is what I know best. If you will be collecting data in another location, consider consulting the Tools of the Trade series within the *Journal of Cognition and Development*. In this series experts provide real advice for all sorts of methods, including testing in schools (Alibali & Nathan, 2010) and public locations such as museums (Callanan, 2012).

Coding data

It is important that your data are reliable and the reader of your project is not simply taking your word for it. If your participants' responses are being directly recorded by a computer (e.g. what they enter is reported in the data file or the computer does the eye-tracking) we can generally trust the computer. However, if *you* are recording your participants' responses, even if you are using a computer (e.g. recording looking times), you'll need to report some measure of inter-coder reliability for some amount of your sample (e.g. 20 per cent).

To get your coders reliable, have them practice until they are at least 85 per cent reliable with each other. Do not use these practices as part of your 20 per cent (ideally use footage from an old study using the same general method). Once your coders are reliable, have them code a reliability every 4th or 5th time data are collected. For example, if you need 25 per cent of your sample recoded for inter-coder reliability, every time you've tested four participants, ask your coder to code a reliability. I do not literally mean perform reliabilities on participants four, eight, twelve, etc., you will want to pseudo-randomly select the participants (so each condition is represented equally).

When you have others coding reliabilities for you it is important not to bias them before they code. For example, if you have a tricky participant and are questioning what the participant did (e.g. a bored child, a keyboard that was acting a bit sporadic), simply say, "I need a reliability done, please code F12" but do not say something like, "Please code F12 – I don't think she made clear responses" because that could bias the coder. It may be that the behavior is not as ambiguous to someone more objective than you.

It is also useful to obtain reliabilities at a regular interval (such as once every five participants) because sometimes coders "drift" and become less reliable. This can especially occur if there has been a long lag time since the last time they coded. In addition, sometimes experimenters begin to drift slightly in how relaxed they are and how closely they follow the proper protocol. You are more likely to catch such drift in a timely manner if you are calculating inter-coder reliability on a regular interval and can estimate when the drift started to occur.

There are several methods for coding inter-coder reliability and agreement. They essentially come down to either creating a correlation between the coders or determining a percentage of agreement. Correlation methods are useful for continuous data, such as looking time agreement, but you may need to include other information. For example, in habituation studies it is possible to have a high correlation between two coders, but one coder could be significantly slower than the other on all of the trials. A good place to look for what method to use is a recent paper that used a similar method to the one you are using.

Percentage of agreement is calculated as the number of times the coders agreed out of the number of times they could have agreed and is ideal for dichotomous data or data that can be broken down trial by trial. For example, imagine a study in which mice decide which of two water bottles to drink from at the end of a maze (maybe one has a sugar solution and one has saline). Let's imagine each mouse completes the maze eight times. You recorded mouse F12 drank from the left bottle on trials 1, 3, 5 and 8 and I recorded 1, 3, 5 and 7 (and we agreed the mouse drank from the right bottle on the other trials). We could have agreed on all eight trials, but we only agreed on trials 1–6, so our agreement is 6/8 = 75%. A more conservative percentage of agreement method you can look up is Cohen's Kappa.

When two (or more) coders disagree, some researchers use the original coder's data and some researchers make the coders discuss and come to a consensus. If your lab does not have a policy on what to do here, examine journal articles on your topic to determine what the general method is. Whatever you do, be sure to be consistent throughout the dataset. You cannot go with the original coder for F12 but then make the coders discuss for M7.

For the record

Most experiments include a lot of record keeping – both electronic and in hardcopy. Although boring, (good) record keeping is a highly transferable skill that can be used in many jobs. Good record keeping involves accuracy and also efficiency: you want to find the recorded information quickly. You also want to record the information quickly and make it clear to others who might need to look up the information when you are not there to help them (e.g. someone who starts in the lab after you graduate or your future boss). Below are some helpful tips for maximizing record keeping.

Box 2.7: Confidentiality and anonymity

Keeping data confidential and anonymous aren't the same thing. Anonymizing data (e.g. assigning a participant ID number) will ensure that as you enter and analyze the data neither you nor someone else can look at the data and think, *This is John's data*. In real life it is possible that you might know "this is John's data" because maybe he is your friend so you tested him first because you were still getting the hang of the study and you knew he wouldn't mind if it took you a long time to set up between tasks. But if others were looking over your shoulder there is no way they should be able to know.

Confidentiality ensures that only those who need access actually have access to the data. This might mean keeping your data files password protected (share the password with your mentor in case he or she needs access after you have left the lab), in locked filing cabinets and in rooms that only the lab group can access.

Keeping confidential records also means keeping participants' performance to yourself (e.g., no gossiping: "Only one child scored 100 per cent, but it was Professor Smith's kid, so I'm not surprised."). When I write letters of recommendation to students "has experience keeping confidential records" is among the top transferable skills I find myself mentioning, especially for jobs that require working with vulnerable groups or handling money (because keeping confidential records is a sign you are trustworthy).

Because your participants have the right to withdraw from your study at any time, you may need to keep a secure list that matches up ID numbers to real names (so if someone were to ring up and tell you she wants to withdraw you could find her data and destroy it). Such records should be kept with neither the consent forms nor the data but in a third location. In many areas of psychology data are collected anonymously, such as when participants complete an online survey without providing their names. This may make it difficult to ensure an individual only participates once, but it certainly does facilitate anonymity and eliminates this step.

"Working with research participants called for professionalism in maintaining privacy and keeping clear boundaries. The same professionalism applies personally as a pastor called to maintain the privacy of people in the community along with keeping clear boundaries in order to uphold a safe environment."

—Joe, BA
Pastor

Hardcopy data

Make the data easy to collect and enter

If you're creating some kind of hardcopy form or worksheet that you or the participant will fill out during the session (I call these "datasheets"), a good thing to consider when you create your form is how you will actually enter the data. You want your form to be easy to use during the experiment so errors aren't made and the sessions are not overly long, but you also want the forms to make data entry swift and easy. If you are using a questionnaire, ensure there is enough space for your participants to write legibly (Foreshaw, 2013), which will help both them and you.

For example, I once conducted a study in which each (child) participant completed four types of test trials (two trials per type for eight total test trials). I counterbalanced the order of the eight test trials across participants because I didn't want the two trials for each type to occur back-to-back. But when it came to entering the data I needed to know what type of trial each trial was. Instead of simply numbering the trials, I also included a code for myself on the datasheet near the trial number, so when I entered the data I could easily pair up the trials.

If you are varying the locations of stimuli (e.g. if the target is left or right), consider if you really need to keep those locations on your datasheet. For example, in most of my word learning studies children choose one of three objects (left, middle, right). Instead of putting the objects where they will appear for the child on the sheet, the sheet has an additional column where we write L, M, or R for where to put the target. We have two kinds of targets and by doing this we can keep all type 1 targets in one column and all type 2 targets in another column. When it comes time to enter the data we just have to count how many words in each column are circled.

Box 2.8: Participant ID numbers

Participant ID numbers are like Social Security (National Insurance) numbers: each participant should have only one ID number and each ID number should only belong to one participant. ID numbers should never repeat, even if the participant's data become excluded.

ID numbers help keep your participants' identities confidential and anonymous when you are looking at the data. There are several ways to create anonymous participant ID numbers:

- Some researchers use random alphanumeric numbers like you sometimes get when you reset your password for a website. This system does an excellent job of keeping participants' identities confidential, but because it is random if you have a typo it can be difficult to go back and determine what the ID number really was. If you want to use this method, you can find a tool to create numbers by searching for "random alphanumeric string generator" online.

- Some researchers use 1M, 2M, 1F, 2F, etc. This can be useful for easily counting how many males and females you have tested, but if you have more than one condition or more than one experiment in a series there is no way to tell what condition "1M" participated in.
- Personally, I like to use a small three-digit code followed by M01, M02, F01, F02, etc. Just like how SSN (NI) prefixes can be informative for knowing someone's region or nationality but not their identity, my three-digit codes reveal what condition the participants were in. For example, if I were conducting a study in which one group of participants read a traditional (paper) book and another group used an e-reader my codes might be PAP (paper) and EBK (e-book). Also, by keeping the count number at the end (i.e. M01 instead of 1M), if I sort my data-entry file by code I can easily keep the male and female participants separate and count them quickly.

Whenever possible, design your datasheets so that they only take up one side of paper, which makes data entry faster. But don't cram so much information onto that one side that you can't read what you or the participant wrote. You may need multiple pages if you won't have enough space to write legibly on one side (see also Foreshaw, 2013).

Design your datasheets so you could perfectly recreate each trial. You will want to know exactly what and where the stimuli were. You may or may not want to enter the data at this basic level, but if there are issues later you will be glad that you can look back. It is easier to record more data than you enter than it is to go back and rewatch videos, and it is much easier to enter more data than you need for the analyses than to go back through and add more information to the data file later.

Box 2.9: Photocopying

Photocopiers are like jumper cables (jumper leads): everyone gets the general concept, but it's likely that you have never needed to use them before (especially in the age of online journal articles). Here is what you need to know.

You may need to log in with a fob or a special ID number and password. I find the log-in process to be the thing that's the most different between different photocopier models, so the first time it's worth it to find someone to show you how to log in on your copier. You will also likely have to log out – this is important so others aren't using your lab's account and paper quota!

If you are copying several pages of regularly sized paper, there is usually a feeder on the top that you can put the paper into. If you are copying something single-sided, you may want to do a test to see if the paper needs to face up or down. Once the paper is in the feeder, you will have to touch a "copy" button but then the machine will do the work for you.

It is worth taking a moment to look through the menu on your copier. You should find options not only for choosing the number of copies to make but also for stapling individual copies and changing the number of pages. For example, you can make a double-sided copy of a single-sided original (this is often depicted with icons that look like pages with lines on them, usually with arrows to show before → after). Many copiers have an option to scan something in (using the feeder) and save it as a PDF file. This can be extremely helpful for archiving data. There are usually drawers for different sizes of paper, but the copier will select the right paper automatically. It is useful to know where these drawers are in case you have to refill them.

If you are copying something small and fiddly (a real book, a receipt), lift the big lid and place the item on the glass and close the lid as much as possible. You will have to touch a "copy" button for each page or each receipt. This can take a long time, so it is polite to do this at a time when few people need the copier. When copying books, it is helpful to make a test copy to check the size is OK. Depending on the size of the book you may want to go to the menu and change the zoom or "ratio" so both of the open book pages fit onto one sheet of paper. For small books I sometimes place plain scrap paper around the edges on the glass so there is a margin around the book and not an inch or two of black that uses excess toner and can't be used for notes. One of my mentors gave me a tip for book chapters: she recommended copying the title and copyright info pages of the book and stapling those at the end of the chapter so you can go back and identify what book "Chapter 3" was in.

A final tip: do not unplug or turn off a photocopier. You do not want to be responsible for wiping the machine's memory! If something is going wrong and you want to unplug, seek assistance from someone in your departmental office.

Keep the data organized

Ensure your participants' ID numbers and conditions are on every page of the hard copy data. If the data get dropped and strewn across the floor or photocopied this will save you loads of time. Using pen instead of pencil will also make the handwritten copies much clearer if photocopied.

You can store data in folders, document boxes or binders. If you choose binders you can either separate each participant's data with a divider or you can put each into a page protector (document wallet). Personally, I use the latter because hardcopy data are prone to tearing if I page through them frequently.

"Try entering data after each session is complete. That way you never fall behind, and don't get confused about what data you have or haven't entered."

—Kerri, BSc
Mental Health Recovery Worker

Electronic data

Keep the data file organized

Eventually all data will get to the electronic stage because you'll use a computer to analyze it. Chapter 4 includes several tips for using the computer when you are entering and preparing to analyze your data.

However, if your data are originating in electronic form (i.e. you are collecting data on a computer), consider as you plan your study the information you will want to have later when you do sit down to analyze your data. You may want to name your stimuli differently depending on the trial type so it is easier to identify if participants are seeing celebrity-face-before the treatment or celebrity-face-after the treatment. Also keep your variable names as informative as possible. Many computer software packages are extremely sensitive to case (read: capitalization), so you will want to be very diligent in being consistent throughout – you do not want your software treating Accuracy and accuracy as two different measures. If you do have two different accuracy measures, names like AccuracyMasked and AccuracyUnmasked will be more informative later. If you do abbreviate something for yourself (e.g., AccMask and

AccUnmk), record that in your lab notebook (p. 24) so you can figure out later what it is or pass that information on to someone else. A good tip is to just pick either all lowercase or All Uppercase and stick with that system.

Back up the data

And then, back it up again. Your data are your project. You do not want to lose your data. Get into the habit of regularly backing up your data now, and even consider two forms of back-up such as an electronic hard drive and a cloud service.

Additional good habits to start now

There is a lot of record keeping in "the real world" outside the lab. This is good because it means you will really be able to put your record-keeping skills to use after your project is completed. In addition to the specific tips above, here are some good habits to start now.

From A to Z

Alphabetize everything you can, and put things listed by numbers in order too – there really is nothing faster. For data I like to follow the rule "ladies first" and keep all of my female participants' data in sequence, then all of my male participants' data. It makes finding things So. Much. Faster.

Embrace color

Outside of the lab, color-coding is surprisingly common: traffic signs, available seats when you book a flight, retail hangers for different-sized clothes, etc. There is good reason: color helps us identify things quickly. For example, imagine you are running multiple conditions of an experiment (e.g., control, experimental) and storing the information in binders. By having each binder a different color, you can immediately see at a glance that you are in fact grabbing the right binder. If you are working alone, this might not seem like a big deal, especially if you really are only dealing with two binders. But if you are part of a team, for example if there are several students in your lab group working on different studies, color-coding allows you to delegate to anyone. You can ask anyone, "Can you please bring my red binder to the lab meeting?" but not everyone will understand, "Can you please bring the binder for the higher memory capacity condition to the lab meeting?"

"Color coding works really well for me as I am a more visual person and can remember things when they are associated with colors, but following a set filing structure makes my brain ache. I think that finding an organizational structure that worked best for me in my own work was the greatest learning tool here and something that I have transferred to the workplace. However, learning to work with and adapt to others' organizational tools is definitely a useful skill to develop as when you move from place to place you will need to be flexible to be able to fit into the new pattern of working."

—Rosa, BSc
Senior Program Manager (Charity Sector)

In my lab, one of the ways we use color-coding is to identify excluded data, so that we can find the "good" data faster during data entry and we can go through all of the excluded data when we write the participants paragraph of the method section. To color-code the excluded data, I have created an "attrition cover sheet" (see Box 2.10) that is photocopied in the ugliest color I can find! Attrition (number of participants tested but whose data are not included in the analyses) needs to be reported in the methods section but is something you really want to keep to a minimum because it can raise serious concerns. For example, if you are excluding a lot of data because your participants cannot do the task, perhaps the task is too difficult and your sample of participants who can do it are no longer representative of the population. Therefore, I make the attrition cover sheet ugly on purpose because it is something we want to see as little of as possible. It then becomes really obvious which data is "good" (clean, white data sheets) and which is not good (e.g. goldenrod).

Box 2.10: Recording attrition

One thing I have found helpful for record keeping is making an "attrition cover sheet" to go in front of data that is being excluded. This is helpful both for quickly identifying data that either does not need to be entered or needs to be entered somewhere special. It is especially helpful for writing the participants paragraph where attrition is reported (e.g. "Three additional children were tested but their data excluded due to . . ."). The one we use in my lab has a place at the top to record the participant ID, date of test, study, experimenter and the person filling out the form (who might not be the experimenter). Then, there is a series of boxes to check/tick for the common reasons a child's data might be excluded from the analyses (e.g. child did not finish the study, the experimenter did something wrong, the parent interfered). There is also a box labeled "other." Next to the boxes there are spaces to elaborate (e.g. "child would not continue after trial 5").

If you ever experience the loss of a participant's data, it will likely be fresh in your mind for a few days, but by the time the study is over, why a particular participant was excluded may not be so memorable. Records like this can really help jog your memory. Also, on occasion participants are "re-included," for example if you decide that even infants who did not habituate can be included or a particular exclusion criterion was too strict. Such records can help you identify who to re-include.

Places, everyone!

I hope you have heard someone say, "A place for everything and everything in its place" before. If not, it's a great motto! Find a place to keep all of the papers, stimuli and tools you use regularly so you know where to go when you need them. Keep things you use more frequently in easy-to-access locations and things you use more rarely in the less-easy-to-access spaces.

A further tip is to keep things where you use them to minimize motion waste (Liker, 2004). For example, if you reimburse participants in the waiting room or reception area, keep the reimbursement forms in the waiting room instead of the coding room; if you grab your clipboard before you leave the coding room, keep the clipboards by the door, not across the room; if you take out parking permits when you take out the consent forms, keep the new permits by the consent forms and not in another drawer.

Finishing your project and exiting the lab

When you finish your project, it is good practice to give your supervisor your data files, if the supervisor does not already have the originals or copies. You may also want to send an email explaining where you put everything and what your files are called (especially if you are working in a large lab group). You may also want to give your supervisor your lab notebook or a copy (p. 24), especially if there is a chance he or she will help you to write-up your project for publication (p. 140). Do not take anything with you. First, it may not be ethical to store data off-site (depending on the guidelines from your ethics committee and how you claimed you would store the data). Second, someone else in the lab group may need your materials to finish or follow up your project if it will be published (e.g. a reviewer might ask for something that requires looking through the footage again). Finally, anything you used that you did not pay for yourself is technically property of the university (whether it was bought from university funds or external grant funds).

Transferring these skills

The focus of this chapter has been on organizational and communication skills you will use frequently, perhaps daily, during your research. We've covered several forms of record keeping: your own notes (lab notebook), records you need for reference (journal articles) and records you will collect (data). Clearly, those are skills you could end up needing in almost any job. Managing large amounts of information is another highly useful skill. Organizing materials so you can easily find authors' names, dates and experiment details isn't all that different from organizing materials so you can find client names, dates and wedding details (as an example).

In many jobs you will have some task that needs to be done semi-regularly but not frequently enough that it becomes easy to remember all of the steps (e.g. an annual safety check or producing a quarterly budget report for shareholders). You can use your procedure-writing and lab notebook skills to create a document you can refer back to so you don't need to remember all the steps – you can also use these skills to make instructions and training guides for others. If you have *already* made instructions and training guides for others, you can highlight this in your job application materials.

Much of this chapter focused on communication skills: effective emailing, cold calling, canvassing strangers, finding your target group. Skills like these are very useful in sales. Even if your job has nothing to do with finding clients and selling something, you may still find yourself ringing strangers for the first time or crafting an email that you need to get answered promptly.

References

Alibali, M., & Nathan, M. J. (2010). Conducting research in schools: A practical guide. *Journal of Cognition and Development, 11*(4), 397–407. doi: 10.1080/15248372.2010.516417.

Callanan, M. A. (2012). Conducting cognitive developmental research in museums: Theoretical issues and practical considerations. *Journal of Cognition and Development, 13*(2), 137–51. doi: 10.1080/15248372.2012.666730.

Foreshaw, M. (2013). *Your Undergraduate Psychology Project.* Chichester, UK: British Psychological Society and John Wiley & Sons Ltd.

Henrich, J., Heine, S. J., & Norenzayan, A. (2010). The weirdest people in the world? *Behavioral and Brain Sciences, 33*(2–3), 61–83. doi: 10.1017/S0140525X0999152X.

Hollich, G. J., Hirsh-Pasek, K., Golinkoff, R. M., Brand, R. J., Brown, E., Chung, H. L., . . . Rocroi, C. (2000). Breaking the language barrier: An emergentist coalition model for the origins of word learning. *Monographs of the Society for Research in Child Development, 65*(3), v–123. doi: 10.1111/1540-5834.00090.

Horst, J. S., & Samuelson, L. K. (2008). Fast Mapping But Poor Retention By 24-Month-Old Infants. *Infancy, 13*(2), 128–57. doi: 10.1080/15250000701795598.

Liker, J. K. (2004). *The Toyota Way.* New York: McGraw-Hill.

Markson, L., & Bloom, P. (1997). Evidence against a dedicated system for word learning in children. *Nature, 385*(6619), 813–15.

Mervis, C. B., & Bertrand, J. (1994). Acquisition of the Novel Name Nameless Category (N3c) Principle. *Child Development, 65*(6), 1646–62.

Spielberg, S. (Writer). (1998). *Saving Private Ryan*: Dreamworks Distribution.

3 All in good time (management)

Here is a confession: I love doing nothing. For me the ideal day would be one where I could wake up, take my time enjoying good coffee and have nothing that I must get done that day: total freedom to do anything and lots of time to spend with those I care about without burdens like "but before we do that, I have to. . . ." This is why I care about time management: I want to get my work done effectively so I have more time outside of work and can enjoy it guilt-free.

People use the phrase "time management" like it's one word, one thing. But it is really much more than that. In fact, it's at least two things: knowing what to do and when to do it. Or put another way, setting goals and completing the tasks that lead to those goals.

Good time management skills can help you complete your project on time with minimal stress and later help you when you start your first job and have to learn things quickly while staying on top of the tasks your boss gives you.

Checklists

Checklists are so powerful for getting things done effectively that there is even a manifesto (Gawande, 2011)! In conducting research, I use checklists for three reasons. First, if I have something written down on a trusty list I can forget about it until I get there. For example, if I make a list of all of the statistical tests I need to do for my paper's results section, I can just forget about it until I sit down to write the results section. I don't have the stress of "Wait! Test for different types of errors in the two conditions! Will I remember that? Oh, I should remember to use Chi-Square for that because the data are categorical and I must remember not to do a t-test. Must. Remember. This. Analysis." Instead, I can remain calm and move my thoughts and energy onto something else. Also, if I do suddenly think of an additional, related idea, I know where to put that information so that I can soon forget about it too.

I also use checklists because it feels so great to tick things off. Simple but true. It feels like you are moving forward, being productive and that something is happening. When I have a checklist of things to put into my results section, for example, I get a sense of accomplishment when I check a couple of things off – even if I haven't accomplished writing the whole section.

> "Making lists is the best way of breaking down a huge task. Include everything on the list – even the small jobs. It really helped me feel like I was in control and also to end the working day on a high, knowing I had ticked off a chunk of work. Keeping organized and knowing what I had done, that I was still on track with the long-term schedule and that I had a plan for the next day (i.e. the rest of the list!) helped me to switch off and rest at night."
>
> —Sam, BSc
> Life Skills Recovery Worker, NHS

Keep in mind, however, that the more baby steps are on your checklist and the more opportunities you have to tick things off for that happy feeling, the longer your checklist will initially appear. Take a look at the two checklists in Figure 3.1. Both checklists cover what needs to be done. Aaron's checklist is short (write method section, create apparatus figure), but John's checklist looks longer and more intimidating even though he isn't necessarily planning to do more than Aaron. However, John will be able to check more things off more frequently, thus getting a sense of where he is in the process and moving forward. Importantly, because John has a more detailed list, he is less likely to accidentally skip something, like adding a statement about ethical approval.

The third, and perhaps most important, reason why I highly recommend checklists, is to avoid skipping steps. When I started conducting

John's Checklist
Write Method Section:
  ✓ Participants Paragraph
  ✓ Statement About Ethical Approval
  ✓ Stimuli & Apparatus Paragraph
  _ Create Apparatus Figure
  ✓ Info About Procedure
  ✓ Info About Counterbalancing
  ✓ Coding Paragraph

Aaron's Checklist
  ✓ Write Method Section
  _ Create Apparatus Figure

Figure 3.1 Example checklists

research, I was very concerned about failing to remember all of the things I needed to tell parents when I went over the consent forms and gave them the paperwork they were to complete while I tested their children. I even went so far as to write for myself a little checklist on a sticky note that I put on the consent form and referred to as I talked to the parents while obtaining consent.

Soon after, I was able to design my own consent forms. I included nice boldface subheadings on the consent form. Now, I could make a more professional impression by secretly using the consent form subheadings as a checklist. I simply pointed to each subheading as I confidently told the parents at CONFIDENTIALITY that their children's records would be kept confidential and nonidentifying subject numbers would be used and at VOLUNTARY that they, or their children, could decide to stop the study at any time for any reason, etc. Now, the only thing I had to remember before giving the parents the consent form to read in full was the instructions for their paperwork, which I eventually memorized with practice.

Box 3.1: Datasheets as checklists

Have you ever driven or biked somewhere, arrived and forgotten how you got there? You obviously drove fine, but as an experienced driver you didn't need to focus on each turn. Or maybe you have read a journal article, turned page after page and later realized you had actually stopped paying attention and were only going through the motions as your eyes scanned left-to-right and top to bottom on each page. Depending on how many participants you have tested as you read this, you may or may not believe me that someday testing participants will become just as automatic. It is actually rather easy to find your mind wandering and drifting while you are testing your 40th participant. As you can imagine, this is where mistakes can be made. Are you really on trial 14? Clearly, you have the stimuli for 13 in front of yourself, so you must have done that one, but what about trial 12?

If you are administering a task where you are presenting a participant with individual trials (not a computerized task or questionnaire), it's good to get in the habit of checking off each trial as you go. Then, this ticking can also become automatic, so if you ever find yourself suddenly on trial 14 with little or no memory of anything that happened after trial 1 you can feel at ease knowing that you did those trials because they are checked off.

Calendars

Keeping a calendar is essential when you are setting up appointments with your supervisor and your participants. You should be familiar with the basics of a calendar; after all, it is simply a place to record when you need to be somewhere or do something. But knowing how to use a calendar effectively can save you a lot of time and effort.

"I would be useless at time management without my diary/ calendar! I find it so useful to see visually how much time I have to do something."

—Emilly, MSc
Research Assistant

Your first decision will be to decide between a hardcopy, paper calendar (diary) or a softcopy, electronic calendar, which is probably online (e.g. Outlook, Google). The advantages of paper calendars are that they look nice and you can doodle on them. The advantages of electronic calendars are much more numerous.

First, you can visualize how long things will take. You can do this to an extent with a paper calendar, for example by drawing arrows and boxes, but where you have blocks of time is much more obvious with an electronic calendar. The computer (or smartphone) can also do the work for you so you don't have to waste time drawing boxes and arrows.

This ability to visualize my time is why I switched to electronic calendars myself. As a student I became frustrated trying to imagine how I was going to get all of my work done because I couldn't get a good sense of where I had free time when I relied on a paper calendar. I switched at the end of my undergraduate degree and never looked back. Take a look at the two calendars in Figure 3.2. Even though the schedules are the same, it is much easier to see that the students have 2.5 hours free in the afternoon and 90 minutes free at the end of the day when you look at Anne's electronic calendar.

Second, you can color-code your appointments. Again, you can do this to an extent with a paper calendar and a highlighter or pretty pens, but again, this will take up your time (and imagine the frustration when you don't have your red pen with you when you need it!). Color-coding your appointments gives you a sense of what you need to do without

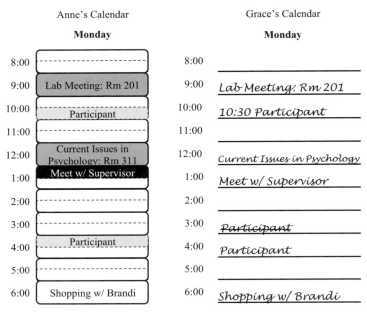

Figure 3.2 Example calendars

you reading the specifics that moment. For example, if all of your experimental sessions are purple, you can just look at today and see you have three purple items: you quickly know that you have three sessions for your experiment. This is really handy if you meet with your supervisor and he asks you how many more participants you have lined up. Unless you are testing a very specific population or conducting an extensive longitudinal study your supervisor is unlikely to want to hear or see the names of your participants. "Three later today, seven by the end of the week" is most likely the kind of response he will want.

You can also easily repeat events. For example, if you have a lab meeting every week (or a team meeting every week once you start your next job) you can easily tell the computer to repeat the meeting every week when you set up the first appointment in the series. It is much more tedious to flip pages and rewrite "lab meeting, lab meeting, lab meeting" over and over again.

If an appointment moves you can also literally move it with an electronic calendar. Again, it is much faster to edit an appointment electronically than to erase it, cross it out or white it out on paper. If your mentor surprises you by saying something like, "I think we'll need at least ninety minutes to look through your analyses" you can also easily extend the time of the appointment.

Online calendars can also be checked anywhere you have an Internet connection. This is a huge advantage if you are suddenly walking between lectures and need to change an appointment or if you are planning your day when you're sitting on the bus into campus. Once when I was a PhD student, the FBI quarantined our psychology building and no one was allowed in or out for several days (don't worry, everyone was fine). I was so glad my lab was using an electronic calendar and could update participants! My friend's lab was still using a paper-based calendar so everyone had to take shifts waiting all day at the entrance just in case any participants showed up. And it rained almost every day.

You can also share your calendar with others, which is really useful if you are sharing resources. For example, if you are part of a lab group where multiple people are testing in the same rooms, having a shared calendar everyone can access reduces the number of emails and phone calls back and forth every time someone wants to set up an appointment. Rather than having each lab member sign up for different days, a shared calendar allows you to test any day, and this flexibility may make scheduling participants easier.

"Shared calendars are an easy and great way to know where everyone is/when rooms are free – sounds so simple, but saves soooo much time. My office loved it when I introduced them to this!"

—Kirsten, MSc
Assistant Psychologist, Prison Service

Finally, consider the information you enter into your calendar. You can enter minimal information if that is really all you need: "participant," "meet with supervisor," "presentation skills workshop." Or you can make the calendar work even harder for you by keeping everything you need in one place. For example, note where the appointments will take place, or if you are scheduling a participant note his/her contact information so you can confirm the appointment the afternoon before.

In my lab we also use the "all day" feature in our electronic calendar to note who will be in the lab and when they are available. This is great when we are on the phone and learn we need an extra lab member to babysit a sibling or if someone calls about another experimenter's session and wants to change the time. I use this feature myself to record deadlines in my own calendar.

Setting priorities and deadlines

Work backwards to set deadlines

Imagine you are taking a flight to your favorite city and it departs at 8:00 p.m. tomorrow. What time do you have to leave home? Now, how did you figure that out? Many people will figure it out by working backwards. If the flight departs at 8:00 p.m., depending on the distance to the destination, boarding will be begin at 7:30 p.m. or even 7:00 p.m. How long does it take to walk to your gate from security or the passenger lounge? How long does it take to get through security *when it is busy* at your departure airport? Will you be checking luggage, and if so, how much time will it take to check in? And of course, how long does it take to get to your departure airport *during traffic*?

The way we figured out the time to leave home was by working backwards. In everyday life we sometimes remember to work backwards, like when we are timing a trip to the airport. But in research, it is easy to just think about where we are now and move forward and to not necessarily think about the goal and work backwards.

Working backwards is a great way to make sure you aren't scrambling at the end trying to fit everything in. One of my all-time favorite books is *The 7 Habits of Highly Effective People* (Covey, 1989), and perhaps my favorite habit is, "Begin with the end in mind." To start thinking backwards, visualize the end. It probably looks like submitting a dissertation that looks like a journal article manuscript. It will include the standard sections (abstract, introduction, methods, results, discussion, acknowledgements, references), but there is more to it than that. It will also include data that have been analyzed, figures that have been made, participants who have all been tested, counterbalancing that has all been completed, stimuli that has been created – and hopefully it will not be the first draft but will have gone through a few rounds of revisions. By thinking about where you are now and where you want to end up (the end) you can determine the intermediate steps and then assign deadlines to these steps.

If you create a timeline or set of deadlines of when you would like to complete each step, it is good to talk this over with your supervisor. He or she will have a better idea about how long each of these steps takes in your research area. For example, I often have students suggest intermediate deadlines that are a bit unrealistic because recruiting and testing children takes longer than students first realize when they haven't done it before. Similarly, I also sometimes remind students of things they can do in parallel. You cannot really make your figures before you have collected all of your data, but you can write your method section while you are still collecting data (because your methods will not change).

> "One thing that I believe helped to alleviate a great deal of stress, and undoubtedly increased the quality of my work, was having to meet incremental deadlines during my final year project. This was vital in preventing any last-minute rushes and enabled me to submit my thesis a week before the deadline – with very little stress or anxiety."
>
> —Lauren H., BSc
> PhD Student

Order of operations

Do you remember in math(s) class learning about order of operations? In mathematics some things have to be done in a set order, for example multiplication before addition. When you are thinking about the intermediate deadlines you have to meet, keep in mind order of operations. For example, you have to recruit your participants before you can test them. But there are also some things you can do in parallel. Identifying these things can help you to make the most of your time. At home, for example, you might set the table while the water for your pasta is boiling so that you can eat dinner that much earlier (and your pasta doesn't get cold).

One way to visualize things that must be done in sequence and things that can be done in parallel is by creating a Gantt chart. This kind of horizontal bar graph will show when different subtasks will start and end and can also show dependencies. For example, your Gantt chart might look something like Figure 3.3.

Having a visual like this can make it easier to see how the steps fit together and what you can work on at the same time. This is a good way to set priorities, to see what is more important and what has to come first.

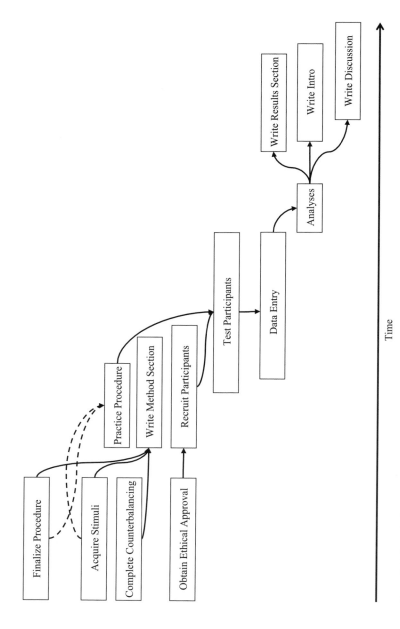

Figure 3.3 Example Gantt chart

"Overall, I feel the ability to manage time has been the most important skill I have developed from working on my final year project.
Recognizing and managing a great deal of responsibilities, alongside prioritizing tasks at hand, is something I have to do myself
but also support others with."

—Naureen, BSc
Education Center Manager

Getting the work done

Upfront work

Sometimes it is worth it to do more work up front to save time later.
For example, one summer as a student I was once an intern at a public
relations company. I regularly needed to ring the same list of magazine
editorial offices. One afternoon, I looked up all of their numbers and
made a list for myself so I didn't have to look them up again and could
just get on with it. I'm sure I saved more time than the time I initially
spent getting things in order.

"It's really important to do a little bit every day. Then it does not
seem to be an insurmountable challenge. If each day you set yourself to do at least, for example, half a page then it does not weigh
on your mind."

—Tash, BSc
Senior Occupational Therapy Assistant

When doing research, it really pays off to take more time initially to
set things up correctly in order to save time later. For example, if you
are running a study where you are recording responses and then entering them into Excel or SPSS later, think about how you are going to
enter the data and what you will need to know and design your testing sheets based on that. For instance, a lot of my students run studies
where we give children multiple toys on a tray and ask them to take one.
I design our testing sheets so that the target (correct) objects are always
in the right-hand column, even though the objects are set on the tray in

different locations. We circle the object the children choose. Then, when we want to enter the data, we just have to count how many items are circled in the right-hand column. If the objects were listed in the order they appear on the tray, it would take a lot more time to figure out how many correct ones the children picked (though you could make the correct choice bold or underlined).

Sometimes it's not just good to know how well your participants did but also what kind of errors they made. If you only record your participants' final scores (e.g. 75 per cent correct), you would have to go back and watch each video if you decided you wanted to report about the errors. If you have designed your testing sheets to record what responses participants gave, rather than simply overall score, then you will be well-prepared and potentially save hours of time (don't ask me how I know!).

Similarly, imagine if you wanted to know if one measure, set or trial type was easier/harder than the rest. You would thank yourself later that you took the time to design your testing sheets so you could record scores for each item than if you had to go back rewatch all of your sessions if someone asked you to confirm there was no effect of set. It is a lot easier to record, but not enter, these intermediate scores than have to go back to figure them out later.

Another area where you can save time by doing some work up front is organizing the paperwork you need to actually run your study. If you have to give individual participants multiple documents (e.g. consent forms, questionnaires, payment sheets), consider taking the time to sort them into "participant packs." Then, instead of taking the time to pull out each document from separate folders when you set up or your participant shows up, you have everything paper-clipped together so you can just grab and go.

"I got into the habit of preparing early for experimental sessions. This way I knew I did not have to worry about anything unexpected and I could focus so I could really get the most out of the sessions."

—Zoe, MSc
PhD student

Know your quadrants

When you are trying to decide how to spend your time, two things that really help are asking yourself: is this task urgent? And, is this task important? Stephen Covey and Roger Merrill demonstrate this idea beautifully in the book *First Things First* (1994), where they discuss four quadrants of time.

For the psychologist, imagine assigning your tasks to cells in a two-by-two design, where one factor is urgency (urgent, not urgent) and one is importance (important, not important). You will be left with four cells (see Figure 3.4). Ideally, you want to be working as much as possible in the second cell, Quadrant 2. Here you are working on things that are both important but not (yet) urgent. Examples would include reading papers for your project, writing methods up ahead of time, entering data before the last minute, etc. There will be times when you will find yourself working in Quadrant 1. Here you are working on things that are both important *and* urgent – for example setting up for an experimental session that is due to begin in only a few minutes, scrambling to get some information together before meeting with your supervisor, etc.

The ultimate goal, in terms of your productivity, is to spend as much time as possible in Quadrant 2, which should also help reduce the amount of time you have to spend in Quadrant 1. In general, a lot of upfront work will be Quadrant 2 activities, which can reduce the number of tasks that slip into Quadrant 1. Also, the more you keep on top of deadlines, the more you can control if you are doing something when it is still in Quadrant 2 or waiting until it is in Quadrant 1. For example, if you know your supervisor likes to have information about how many participants you have tested before each weekly meeting, you could either keep track as you go and jot this information down the morning of your meeting (or night before if you meet first thing the next day) or you could wait until just a couple minutes before your meeting and find the information then. In both cases you'll have the information ready for the meeting, but the first approach is doing the

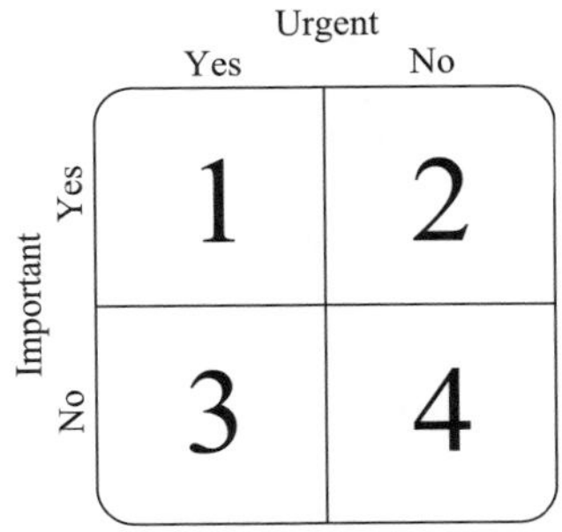

Figure 3.4 Covey and Merrill's (1994) Four Quadrants

task when it is important and not (yet) urgent (Quadrant 2) and the second is waiting until the task is both important and urgent (Quadrant 1). I know which approach I would prefer!

You cannot control everything, especially when you are conducting research with real human subjects and live animals and/or working in a lab group with multiple members. But the more you can do in Quadrant 2, the more you can lower your daily stress levels and the more in control you can feel. Sometimes Quadrant 1 is unavoidable: critical equipment can break down right before your participant arrives and your first participant can be twenty minutes late while the next is ten minutes early. The more time you spend in Quadrant 2, however, the less stressful these situations feel because you don't have to worry about the things in Quadrant 2.

Imagine Katie and Natalie have the same supervisor who wants to see their data in a lab meeting at 4:00. Katie works in Quadrant 2 and generally enters data as she goes, but Natalie has no idea what Katie is on about when she talks about quadrants and just plans to enter the data before the meeting. Imagine some equipment breaks before the experimental session right before the meeting and now they have to get on the phone and find someone who can fix it and figure out what to tell the participant – and while they sort this out they cannot enter their data. Katie will be fine. If she only gets fifteen minutes before the meeting to enter data, she might be able to enter it all because she's been entering the data *before* it was urgent and will only have a few to enter. Absolute worst-case scenario, she can probably just explain, "The equipment broke. It was more urgent to sort that out before the participant came, so I didn't get all of my data entered. However, I do have data entered for the eighteen participants I tested before today." Natalie, unfortunately, will be in an entirely different situation.

As a mentor, it's great when students can tell me things while they are in Quadrant 2, before they get into Quadrant 1. For example in my lab we sometimes have participants come by bus or train. When they do, we reimburse them with cash, which I have to get by going into the campus bank, at times when the bank is open for business. When students can tell me ahead of time, "We're running low on cash. We will need some by the end of tomorrow," it is significantly easier for me to get back to them with what they need before it's too late. In contrast, when students wait until the last minute to tell me, "We don't have any cash left. We have someone coming in by bus at 2:30," I also find myself in Quadrant 1, scrambling to make a good, professional impression.

Box 3.2: Staying in Quadrant 2

There are a lot of little day-to-day things that go into running a successful study. I don't necessarily mean a study that yields significant data, but a study that is completed on time (or even a little early to allow for more polishing and editing of the final project paper). In order to stay on top of things and keep things from morphing into Quadrant 1 territory, I have done three easy, practical things.

First, I have made some lab checklists that lab members review on a regular basis. For example, I am the only lab member with access to the room where the office supplies are kept (departmental policy). When we run low on something I can drop what I am doing, walk all the way around the building and get what we need. Or we can quickly look over the checklist at the start of our lab meetings so I can pick things up in between tasks when I am on that side the building.

Second, a student suggested we have signs in our folders with paperwork. Instead of just having a hanging folder with all of the blank consent forms (which you might have even if you have some participant packets), we have a folder of consent forms but in front of the last consent form we have a bright yellow sheet of paper that says THIS IS THE LAST CONSENT FORM: PHOTOCOPY ME! It can be a real nightmare to find out you are out of consent forms right before a participant is coming, especially on a Saturday when the photocopier isn't available (don't ask me how I know that either!).

Finally, I have made worksheets that are very similar to checklists for student-mentor meetings. On one half of the page there is space to make notes and on the other half there are checkboxes with lines next to them where we can record a task to do, who is supposed to do it and by when. Then, during the next meeting we can check if all of the boxes are ticked.

Thinking about the things you are working on in terms of the quadrants is also useful for identifying Quadrants 3 and 4. Quadrant 3 includes things that are urgent, but they are not actually very important or they are urgent for someone else – for example getting a signature for a small research expense before the person signing goes on vacation.

Quadrant 4 is especially dangerous territory. This is the black hole of things that are neither urgent nor important. Quadrant 4 might include some time you spend online, time spent listening to (boring) stories that don't have a point or reading spam emails. If you find yourself really struggling with this kind of thing there are easy ways to help yourself. For example, there are apps and add-ons for web browsers that you can use that shut down a website or program after a predetermined set time limit, for example Anti-Social or LeechBlock. Some of these add-ons are aimed at adults and others are aimed at parents who want to limit their children's screen-time. You can use either. Such add-ons often include a tedious way to enter at least one password to circumvent the system if you really do need to get back into the program or back onto a website (this can be useful if, for example, you use Facebook as a phone directory). If you do really wonder where your time is going, consider keeping a time journal for one week (Vanderkam, 2011).

Actually taking time out for yourself though – relaxing and recharging – that is not Quadrant 4. Everyone needs to recharge, so if you really are recharging your batteries, that is very likely Quadrant 2.

"I think it's important to make sure you have time for yourself (*not partying*). I remember when I was at university – especially in the final year – having so much work to do all the time that I didn't have much time to myself to relax, recharge my batteries or do something other than university. I think sometimes it's really important to make sure you do have that time so then you are refreshed and stay motivated."

—Lauren L., BSc
Teacher

Understand when perfectionism doesn't matter

There are a few things I think we can agree that you want to do: work up front, spend as much time in Quadrant 2 as possible and generally do a great job. A sometimes-hidden pitfall of this is perfectionism.

Now, I love attention to detail. That's often what separates the mediocre from the great or the very good from the exceptional (compare the red hair of Ariel in *The Little Mermaid* (Clements & Musker, 1989) to Merida in *Brave* (Andrews, Chapman, & Purcell, 2012)).

Sometimes, however, researchers can get trapped making something perfect that really doesn't have to be. Don't get me wrong: I'm not saying that you shouldn't aim to make things easy to read, visually appealing and neatly organized. However, if you catch yourself polishing and tweaking something for more than about half as long as it took to finish the task, consider if you are really spending your time wisely. For example, if your supervisor wants to know how many male and female participants you have tested, ask yourself if just writing the information down by hand on a piece of paper will be sufficient or if you really need to create a table in Word or Excel.

Set aside the time

When I was writing my undergraduate dissertation there came a moment when I realized that if I didn't do something I wasn't going to make the deadline. My other classes and my jobs just got in the way. I had to do something, and my solution was to schedule time with myself.

Now, years later, I have seen that many successful people are successful because they made themselves set aside the time to get their writing done. For example, in his memoir, Stephen King (2000) writes about how he had to set aside time to get his writing done back when he was a teacher before his writing career took off.

As a student what worked for me was to set aside time at the beginning of the day. Mondays through Thursdays I made myself get up one hour earlier than I normally would (I let myself have Fridays off). For that first hour I was up I didn't let myself check email or go online. I did make coffee (sometimes you need some kind of incentive to get out of bed). I'll be honest with you. Some days it was a little bit of a struggle to make myself get up early so I could write a challenging passage. But I kept my eye on the prize: I wanted to do well on my dissertation and I didn't want to come "this close" and not make the deadline. I also reminded myself that it was temporary. I would only be a student in my final year once. After I handed in my dissertation I wouldn't have to get up this early anymore. Just to be clear, these four extra hours I found by getting up an hour early helped, but I had to work on my project at other times as well. Four hours per week wasn't enough to get my project done well – at least by the time I finally started scheduling time with myself.

A lot of people have a hard time scheduling time with themselves because they think that a small block of time won't be enough to get something done. Even among my colleagues I hear people talk about how they can't wait until they have full days they can set aside to write. It's nice to think about having a full day to do nothing but work on an important project, but it is very unlikely you will have a full day, especially if you are testing individual participants or have classes. When you start a job it is even less likely you will have a full day all to yourself without interruptions or appointments. However, the good news is that people who schedule blocks of time to write regularly, as opposed to waiting until they can do "binge writing," write more – and their writing is better (see e.g. Silva, 2007).

> "Be organized – a key to being effective in completing your final year project with minimal stress. Allocating time to do this is also very important. I felt that having set deadlines that I had to meet kept me on track and organized my priorities."
>
> —Naureen, BSc
> Education Center Manager

You say pomodoro, I say tomato

Have you ever found yourself faced with a rather unpleasant task, but one that you knew you had to get done? In research such tasks might be data entry, statistical analyses, emailing participants, disinfecting the lab, etc. One useful way to tackle these kinds of tasks is the Pomodoro Method.

This method comes from Italy, where kitchen timers are often shaped like tomatoes (*pomodori*). The general idea is to set a timer for a short amount of time (e.g. twenty-five minutes) and commit yourself to doing the task for that long and then allow yourself to take a break. I use this method myself at work, for example when I'm grading papers, and at home, for example when I'm filing papers or spring cleaning. Often tasks that are not intrinsically motivating are much more appealing when we can tell ourselves, "OK, I can do this for just fifteen minutes." It might not seem like much, but that's fifteen minutes more completed than if you had just surfed the Internet, watched TV or done whatever else you would have been doing with that time. In fact, a person can get so much done in fifteen minutes that there is even a best-selling book for PhD students called *Writing Your Dissertation in 15 Minutes a Day* (Bolker, 1998). Sometimes, people even find that once they start and get into a task they are happy to keep working for a little longer. Maybe after ten minutes you might decide you can work until fifteen before you let yourself take a break.

As a psychologist, I like this method because I know we can only really concentrate on something for about forty-five minutes. The longest I ever let myself go without a break is about fifty minutes.

Taking breaks is also important for ergonomic reasons. It is important to give your eyes a break from staring at a computer screen for too long or your back a break from sitting still for too many hours. A colleague in an office across the hall from mine sets his phone to go off once every

"It is very important to take regular breaks. The best way of doing this is by getting into a routine and by making sure this is a routine which works for you. I know I am not a morning person, so I embraced this and worked from lunchtime onwards, right through the evening and into the night. Others may think it is not healthy to be working at 22:00 or 23:00, but if this is what works for you, then that is fine. I ensured I had regular breaks (e.g. a set coffee break in the library café, dinner with friends, scheduled phone calls, ten minutes to use the Internet/check personal emails)."

—Sam, BSc
Life Skills Recovery Worker, NHS

sixty minutes. When it goes off, he doesn't take a real break but stands up and stretches and moves around for a minute. I try to remind myself to take a walk a few times each day (e.g. refill my water bottle, get an afternoon coffee). This forces me to stop staring at my computer screen and makes my eyes focus on something else. Before I started doing this I used to get terrible headaches from too much screen time.

Making the most of downtime

When you are conducting research where you are testing individual participants, there are often small gaps of time in between participant sessions. This downtime can seem like a real waste of time, especially as you see it add up. When I was a student our policy was to wait for our participants at the front entrance of the psychology building. We waited from fifteen minutes before the scheduled appointment time (in case the participant was early) to fifteen minutes after the appointment time. There were several participants who would arrive up to fifteen minutes late, which could mean thirty minutes of downtime. If a participant didn't show up, I could have up to another forty-five minutes to fill until it was time to wait for the next one. I soon realized it was in my best interest to figure out something to do with all of that time. Some of the ways I used that time was to read journal articles and write to-do lists.

Consider making a list of things you can do during these periods of downtime. By using these secret snippets of time, you can really get a lot done by the end of the day. You can also chip away at some unpleasant tasks if you combine this with the Pomodoro Method discussed above. Box 3.3 gives you some ideas of things you might be able to do during these short intervals.

Box 3.3: Suggestions for filling downtime

Plan your day or week (to-do lists)
Recruit participants (calling, emailing)
Send parking permits, thank-you notes, anything else to prepare to mail
Photocopying
Check inventory for lab supplies/participant thank-you gifts
Restock lab office supplies (printer paper, paper clips, staples)
Order lab supplies online
Enter data or check data entry
Inter-coder reliabilities, coding or transcribing
Start reading a journal article
Search for and download papers to read later
Contact an author or request a paper through interlibrary loan
Print copies of papers to read later if you read hardcopies
Measure your stimuli (if applicable for your methods section)
Work on a presentation (animate a PowerPoint file)
Make notes or flashcards for revision/studying for an upcoming exam
Make a *short* personal phone call (if possible)
Clean the lab (clean instruments, disinfect keyboards, wash toys, etc.)

A few years ago I started keeping a to-do *folder*. Over time it has morphed into an electronic app on my smartphone. When I'm doing something else, like writing, and I think of a small task to do, like make a haircut appointment, I just jot it down on that list (or on a piece of scrap paper and put it into that folder) and then when I have downtime or I'm taking a break, I look through my list of short items to do and see if I can tackle any of them in the time I have. Sometimes, knowing that I don't have very long actually makes the task more appealing. For example, if you have to ask someone else in the department something in person, but you know that person is chatty, it can be helpful if you have to say, "I'm sorry, I can't stay to chat; I have a participant coming in a few minutes. Thank you for answering my question though!"

Location, location, location!

One useful consideration for managing your time is imagining where you will be. Not all locations are equally suited to working on your project. Sure, you can do some brain storming almost everywhere, but you can't always do the smaller jobs like data entry, inter-coder reliability coding or filing.

One tip David Allen gives in his book *Getting Things Done* (2001) is to make different to-do lists depending on where the work will be done. He adds an @ symbol before his lists (which in some software can help put things to the top of the alphabetical list) and then considers where the work can be done. For example, you might have an @Lab list for things you can do in the lab and an @Downtime list for things you can do during downtime or when you don't have a lot of energy to do the mentally taxing parts of your project like writing.

Give yourself a cushion

Remember the airport example from earlier? Did you notice that I imagined security was busy and we were going to the airport during traffic? When you imagine how long it will take to get a (sub)task done, it is very useful to consider it will take longer than it should under ideal circumstances. Very often research takes longer than expected. Sometimes equipment breaks, supplies do not arrive on time, participants cancel and sometimes experimenters get sick or there are family emergencies to attend to. You can't always predict how long research will take, but you can predict it will take longer than originally expected.

That's why it's important to give yourself a cushion. As you are planning your intermediate deadlines, try to add extra time for each subtask.

"Although time management is important throughout the degree, it wasn't until the third year that I actually had to juggle so many things. Usually, deadlines are spaced out nicely over the first two years, but in the final year you have to run your project *and* keep up with your other courses. So it's the first time you are in charge of dividing up your time in that way.

"Don't put anything off ''til next week.' Pretty obvious, but if you need to buy stimuli (for example), get it as soon as you know what you need. It may take a while to find what you need. Same with data collection. The sooner you start, the more time you will have to iron out any problems."

—Matt, BSc
PhD Student

If you are only setting deadlines for writing, try to factor in time to do edits and also extra time just in case. You might need it if you can't get a hold of a key reference, if your mentor doesn't give you comments back on time, if your printer decides to stop working. If you factor in extra time and don't need it, that's a bonus. There is no reason you can't turn your dissertation in early, but you really don't want to turn it in late.

Know thyself

The ancient Greek philosophers were very wise. One of their maxims was inscribed on the temple of Apollo at Delphi: know thyself. When it comes to real-life time management this is very, very important. I hope you get some useful tips from me, your supervisor and others in your lab group, but really it's important for you to decide if these tips will really work for you. For example, I've already told you about how I made myself write on my dissertation most weekday mornings from 6:00 till 7:00 a.m. But I'm a morning person. I can often jump out of bed and be ready to go (especially if there is good coffee as incentive to sit upright). You might not be a morning person. My former student Sam is not a morning person. She primarily worked on her project in the evening and into the night. That wouldn't work well for me, I get too tired after dinner, but it worked well for her. If you know yourself and what your strengths and weaknesses are, then you can plan things at times that fit best with your own body clock.

For example, because I'm a morning person I also have a real slump in the afternoon. Sometimes I set aside tasks that are less mentally taxing for me (e.g. photocopying) and save them for the early afternoon when I'm not at my peak so my writing is extra slow and data entry is more prone to errors. I'm still able to feel like I'm getting things done during these slumps and I'm saving time in the long run because I'm not letting myself do things I wouldn't do well and might have to redo (like data entry). I find that having a list of downtime tasks is really handy for these sluggish times as well. The important thing is to know what will work for you, and if something won't that is OK as long as your research is being done properly, ethically and on time.

Insider tricks of the trade

Multitasking is a myth

People like to believe they are good at multitasking, but it's just not true. There are very few tasks that people can really do at the same time, for example walking and chewing gum, having a conversation while making dinner, letting the washing machine do a load of laundry while reading a journal article. Many times when people think they are multitasking they are really switching rapidly between tasks. Like prunes versus dried plums, task switching just doesn't have a nice ring to it the way multitasking does.

Researchers investigating multitasking have actually uncovered that people are more productive when they do one thing at a time (Ophir, Nass, & Wagner, 2009). This should make sense. If we are really switching between tasks, we are really doing one thing at a time anyway – even if we like to think we are doing email, online messaging and writing a method section at the same time. When we switch between tasks, though, it takes time to reorient and get back on track. "Which sentence was I on? Right, no difference in age between groups. . . ." Over time, the time it takes to reorient builds up. It is ultimately faster – and you are less likely to make mistakes that need correcting – when you just accept that we're all human and we're really just switching between tasks. Embrace the fact that we are already doing one thing at a time. Let the one thing you are doing or the one person you are talking to have all of your attention. Unless, of course, that one thing is laundry or dishes. Go ahead and delegate that to a machine so you can get on with more interesting things.

Save your energy

Have you ever noticed how tiring it is to repeat yourself? Perhaps you had a question and were sent from person to person to find the answer, each time being asked the same questions and providing the same answers. It can be exhausting.

There is a lot of repetition in research, from the items on your to do list to the information you record about your participants. You can save time and energy by reducing how much you record: not by recording less information but by shortening the information you record by leaving things out and abbreviating.

Besides the differences in length, did you notice any other differences in the checklists in Figure 3.1? Except for "Create Apparatus Figure" everything else on John's list was essentially "write ___" but he only lists the items because "write" becomes redundant information when it is all about writing (with the exception of the Apparatus Figure). Importantly, the items make sense without the command "write." There are many occasions when you are doing research when your list will make sense with few words. For example, when recording the reasons why participants' data are excluded from the final sample you can probably record "experimenter error" instead of "excluded due to experimenter error." After all, what else would "experimenter error" mean?

In fact, you can probably cut that down further by abbreviating and recording "E-error." As long as you know that E- refers to experimenter and not equipment you will be fine (maybe EQ- refers to equipment). When I start using abbreviations that are new to me, I record them in the margin of the document, list or file that I need the abbreviation for. This is also very handy when you start a new job and need to know that WENUS stands for Weekly Estimated Net Usage System, as an example (Lembeck, 1995). It is OK to be creative in your abbreviations. Why use EQ-error for equipment error when Q-error would work just as well? When I am hand-writing I sometimes even use Greek letters such as Pi (process) and Delta (development).

Handle paper once

Another immensely helpful tip from productivity guru David Allen (2001) is to only handle paper once. Instead of taking an email or a note to do something and putting it in an intermediate stack to handle later or to file, just handle it now and file it right away. This sounds very simple, but it can take some time to make this a robust habit. This relates to the idea of putting less information into your emails (p. 37): if you ask people for some information they can handle quickly, they are more likely to do it now, rather than to set it aside to do later.

Another way you can save time with paper is to literally handle it less. Try to touch each piece of paper once. If it is in your hand, file it, don't put it in a stack of papers to file later. If you are pulling a piece of paper out of a folder or page protector (document wallet) to write something at the top, don't pull it out all the way, just as far as you need. If you are writing the same thing on multiple pieces of paper, just flip to the corner or half you need instead of moving entire pages.

Spending less time on the phone

Although much participant recruitment now occurs by email and online sign-ups, some researchers still need to ring potential participants by phone. When I was a student I often had set times to call and lots of numbers to ring, so I needed to be quick in between. I observed other students gently hanging up the phone in between, then writing their notes, then getting the next call sheet ready, then picking up the phone – they were noticeably slower, and it looked to me like they were wasting so much time. I thought it was just me until I watched the movie *The Pursuit of Happyness* (Muccino, 2006) in which Chris Gardner, played by Will Smith, complained about the same thing! Chris became a millionaire entrepreneur, but when he started out as an intern in a stock brokerage company, he had to make similar phone calls. He noticed that hanging up between calls by using his fingers saved him eight minutes per day. We've already talked about how a lot can be accomplished in fifteen minutes, so you know eight minutes here and there really will add up.

In addition to saving time hanging up in between calls, use the time when the phone is ringing on the other end. If you have to write down the date and time you called, you can do this while the phone is connecting and starts ringing. You don't have to wait until the phone call is over to record these details. Sometimes I even went so far as to dial the number and then look at the name of the person to ask for while the phone was ringing. Importantly, one reason I could do this is because all of my information was in the same format, so I could look at the same location on every call sheet (this is similar to a visual search task). I could dial, then look at the location for the name and then start writing down the date and time while the phone was ringing.

> "When contacting participants have a checklist of information you need to find out (e.g. age, do they need parking permits). Contacting them a second time for information you missed can look unprofessional."
>
> —Kerri, BSc
> Mental Health Recovery Worker

Use mnemonics to automate your checklists

You can super-charge your checklists by turning them into mnemonics. For checklists that you will turn to multiple times (or will need to know in an emergency), this is a great method for ensuring you remember everything on your list. A mnemonic is often a simple word or phrase where each letter stands for an item you want to remember to check off. For example, a well-known mnemonic for considering if someone is suffering from a stroke is FAST (Face drooping, Arms weak, Speech slurred, Time to call for an ambulance). By using a single letter to represent a whole item on the checklist, the information is condensed and easier to remember as a whole list (this may be reminiscent of chunking from cognitive psychology).

In the very second episode of the medical drama show *House, MD* (O'Fallon & Shore, 2004) the team use the mnemonic MIDNIT (midnight) to make a diagnosis. Each letter stands for something else to consider and helps ensure the team doesn't skip a critical kind of symptom, ranging from metabolic to trauma. In real life, after we had a child, my husband and I discovered that our mornings were a lot more hectic and we were more likely to forget things that caused significant delays when we had to run back home and missed our trains. To help our sleep-deprived selves, we created the mnemonic PICKET: phone, ID [card], coffee, keys, eats and [train] ticket – which we are still using years later.

How do you make a mnemonic? Begin by thinking about the things you want to remember and what they are usually called. If you are lucky, then the list will be short and the initial letters will obviously unscramble to make a nice mnemonic. If this doesn't work, search online for scrabble solvers: websites designed for Scrabble players to enter the letters they have and then get a list of the possible words that can be made from these letters. Usually there is a special symbol for blank tiles. When you do this, be flexible. For PICKET, for example, L for "lunch" wasn't working for me, so I changed it to "eats," which gave me a useful vowel and reminds me of the quirky television chef Alton Brown. Also, if possible, try to avoid repeating a letter; as Dr. House comments on MIDNIT, it is really annoying (and it can slow you down). Ideally, you want to be left with a word you can easily remember and spell.

Sometimes there is information you need to remember for a short time, so it isn't worth it to create a mnemonic, but the information is critical. Maybe you are tasked with shutting down the lab before the university closes for the winter break and you have to remember to shut down all of the computers, unplug other equipment, securely close the windows and ensure the filing cabinets are locked (which you probably want to write down on a traditional checklist). Because you may never need to interact with this once-a-year checklist again, it probably isn't a good use of time to create a cute mnemonic. Another tactic in this case could just be to remember four: there are four major things to do. You could try to link something to four to also remember how many things are on your list (winter break is four weeks long?). Then, when you find yourself standing in the lab with a feeling of, "Is there something I'm missing?" you can remind yourself there were four things to do to jog your memory.

Transferring these skills

This chapter focused on time management and how you can best manage your time to complete your project on time. Importantly, however, these tips on time management are not specific to research. In fact, almost every book I have mentioned was actually written for the business world! A lot of these skills clearly transfer to other jobs. In fact, you might want to think about using these time management skills *to get the job*.

For example, a classic interview question is, "Tell us about a time when you solved a problem/took initiative." You could answer this with a lab anecdote like, "I noticed a problem in the lab where equipment wasn't being turned off at the end of the day [which runs up the utility bills]. I created a simple checklist that could be used by the last member of staff to leave. This checklist is still in use several months later."

Similarly, if you are asked about how you would prioritize your workload if you were working on the Big Account you might talk about "beginning with the end in mind" and working backwards – but that it's also important to have a cushion because sometimes the unexpected happens. You may also be able to give practical examples of how you could implement some of these ideas. You might explain, "I created packs for my participants with everything they needed to know about the study. I'm sure I could put together welcome packs for guests at your hotel."

Once you get the job, you will still need to manage your time (sorry, you'll still only have 168 hours each week). Whenever possible, try to spend your time in Quadrant 2 (Covey, 1989; Covey & Merrill, 1994). If you need to work on a dreaded or tedious task, use the Pomodoro (tomato) Method and remember to have ideas of things to do during downtime. And if you need to create a timeline, consider a Gantt chart so you can see how the steps feed into each other.

References

Allen, D. (2001). *Getting Things Done: How to Achieve Stress-free Productivity.* London: Penguin Books.

Andrews, M., Chapman, B., & Purcell, S. (Writers). (2012). *Brave*: Disney-Pixar.

Bolker, J. (1998). *Writing Your Dissertation in 15 Minutes a Day.* New York: Owl Books.

Clements, R., & Musker, J. (Writers). (1989). *The Little Mermaid*: Disney.

Covey, S. R. (1989). *The 7 Habits of Highly Effective People.* New York: Simon & Schuster.

Covey, S. R., & Merrill, A. R. (1994). *First Things First: Coping with the Ever-Increasing Demands of the Workplace.* New York: Simon & Schuster.

Gawande, A. (2011). *The Checklist Manifesto: How to Get Things Right.* London: Profile Books, Ltd.

King, S. (2000). *On Writing: A Memoir of the Craft.* New York: Simon & Schuster.

Lembeck, M. (Writer). (1995). The One with Two Parts: Part 1, *Friends*: Warner Bros. Television.

Muccino, G. (Writer). (2006). *The Pursuit of Happyness*: Columbia Pictures.

O'Fallon, P. (Writer) & D. Shore (Director). (2004). Paternity, *House, MD*: Universal Studios.

Ophir, E., Nass, C., & Wagner, A.D. (2009). Cognitive control in media multitaskers. *PNAS Proceedings of the National Academy of Sciences of the United States of America, 106*(37), 15583–15587. doi: 10.1073/pnas.0903620106

Silva, P. J. (2007). *How to Write a Lot: A Practical Guide to Productive Academic Writing.* Washington, DC: American Psychological Association.

Vanderkam, L. (2011). *168 Hours: You Have More Time Than You Think.* New York: Portfolio.

4 Make your computer work for you

Computers require maintenance (e.g. upgrades, updates and dusting), so a computer can be "a lot of work." It can be easy to lose track of the fact that the computer's job is to save you from "a lot of work" by actually helping you do your job faster or more easily. My goal for this chapter is to give you ideas of how you can get your computer to work for you now – and later.

Computer software can change quickly. New versions come out even faster than new textbook editions! Because of this speed, I am not always going to be precise about where in Word, Excel, Power-Point, etc., you will find different menu options. If you cannot find a setting I mention, just look through the different menus or look it up online (I've had to do this many times myself as new editions come out).

Because you are likely using the computer for many different tasks (in fact you might use the computer more often than you do *not* use it!), I will first cover file organization, then writing/word processing and finally number crunching (i.e. data entry, preliminary data analysis). Note, creating presentations, figures and tables is covered in Chapter 6.

Computer organization

When I started doing research I literally had a spiral notebook for each study. It was very handy because I could make notes on whatever paper was around and tape that into my notebook. Nowadays I use Word files and give them titles like "Color Study Paper Trail," which is even better because I can use the "find" function to search within the document (Ctrl+f on a PC or Cmd+f on a Mac). For example, I can have Word search for the word *figure* instead of manually turning page after page to find a note like "make a stimulus figure like Smith, 2015 p. 10."

"I made sure I labeled everything, paper notes and electronic documents. This meant that I avoided spending hours looking for things. I also used an "old versions folder." This meant that I did not delete old editions of the report but they were kept separate from the most up-to-date version that I was working on. I also found using the date edited in the title of documents a handy time saver."

—Camilla, BSc
Assistant Psychologist (National Health Service)

What's in a name: naming files and folders

Back when the personal computer was just becoming a popular concept, file names could only be eight characters long and could not include special characters. Those days are long gone. So take advantage of the flexibility you have in naming your files (e.g. instead of *counterbalancing.docx* you can have *counterbalancing design smoking study.docx*). A longer title will enable you to search for several logical words if you accidentally forget what the file is named (e.g. if your file is named *counterbalancing.docx* you may not find it by searching for "design").

Keep in mind that you can also use naming tricks to keep files in a set order. For example I often label sub-folders "[space][space][space] Data Files" so they are at the top of the list when I open the folder. David Allen (2001) is a big advocate for adding @ before file and folder names as another way to keep them in a useful order. I've even used "zzz" at the start of folder names to get them to the bottom of an alphabetized list.

Some people swear by adding dates to file names (e.g. *Smoking Paper Draft [date].docx*). If you think that this system will work for you (or your mentor tells you to do it this way), by all means go all out. Personally, I find the dates really don't help me. Without stopping to concentrate really hard I can't tell you what the date was a week before yesterday, so knowing I wrote something on March 2 isn't going to help me much. Plus, if I want to know the date I wrote something my computer will tell me the "last modified" date for the file.

Instead, I re-save-as and name multiple versions (e.g. *Smoking Paper Draft 3.docx*). It's similar, but I find this system works better. I only renumber a new version if I've made a large change like deleted a whole section, moved paragraphs around, etc. Then, if I made a mistake and want to go back I have the older version saved.

What's in an alias

Sometimes it is not immediately clear where something should be filed (Should the info about figures go in your data folder or your writing folder? Should the company mission statement go in the employee policies folder or the annual meeting with shareholders folder?). Fortunately, you don't need to make duplicates – which can then create a lot of extra work if you don't know which one has the latest edits, so you have to open each one. Instead, when you look at the document icon you can right-click and create an "alias" (on a Mac) or a "shortcut" (on a PC). This will create a new file that you can move to another location. Just be careful if you delete something that you know if you are deleting the alias/shortcut or the original.

Word processing

Autocorrect is actually incredibly smart

I think my favorite time-saving feature of Word is Autocorrect, but not because it fixes words that I frequently write with typos (like teh). I especially enjoy autocorrect because I can create my own autocorrect entries like shortcuts.

For example, when I write papers I frequently use the phrase "novel name referent selection trials," which can be rather annoying because with five words there are many chances to make a typo and with such a long phrase, by the time I have finished typing it I can lose my train of thought or the just-perfect way I wanted to write the end of the sentence. My single solution to both avoiding typos for long phrases and wasting time typing them is to create my own autocorrect entries (when you look at the list of autocorrect words there is an option to add your own).

Autocorrect works by replacing the original text with the corrected text once you hit the space bar. That could be highly problematic if you want it to replace text that can occur on purpose. For example if I wanted "rs" to autocorrect to "referent selection" anytime I wrote phrases like "the authors" or "these behaviors" I would end up with a mess to fix and that would defeat the purpose. So, whenever I add a shortcut into autocorrect I use * before the shortcut (e.g., *rs, *nnrs) because I don't accidentally type *rs in my documents. This really speeds up writing. It also ensures that you never have typos in the phrases you use frequently – if you entered them into autocorrect correctly, of course!

(Note, because you have to hit the spacebar, if the word is at the end of your sentence, you will want to go back to insert a period [full stop] or other punctuation.)

You can also create shortcuts like this on your phone, which can be useful if you frequently text or email the same phrases (e.g. directions to the lab, reminders of appointments, confirmations of client orders).

Spell check is actually . . . not so smart

Here's a confession: I'm a terrible speller. Obviously, as a poor speller I highly recommend *always* enabling spell-check on anything with this capability. But the problem is that even with spell check on you can have spelling (and typo) failures. For example, "trail" will slide right under your spell check's radar even if you mean "trial" because "trail" really is a word. Worse, because it is also a noun, you are unlikely to get a prompt about the grammar either.

My arguably low-tech solution for this kind of problem is to run "find" and "replace" after I write important documents with words I think are potential problems. If "trail" (or another problem word) isn't in your document, your computer will just tell you it wasn't found. If it is in there, the computer can replace it with "trial" (or the other correct word) automatically – just be careful that you spell the replacement word correctly! Sadly, I know of a published journal article where a word was changed from US to UK spelling but there is a typo in that word every time it is used. D'oh!

Box 4.1: References: Make the computer do it

Have you ever typed up a references section? Pretty tedious, right? You and I are not the first people to think so. In fact, there are several pieces of add-on software designed to make the task easier. If there is a copy of a reference software package (e.g. EndNote, RefWorks) in your lab, ask if you can use a copy. Look online for video tutorials or ask a postgraduate student, post-doc or your mentor to show you how to use it. If possible, try to use something your supervisor is already using so you can turn to him or her for help.

Such software packages "magically" create your reference list at the end of your document (well, actually you have click and add references in the text, but the software formats it), figuring out which order all of the papers by the same author go. What I find even more useful is that the software keeps track of how many times I've referred to something so I don't need to wonder if a reference should be "et al." or still with all three authors' names listed.

A word of caution: it's really important when you start using such software to type in authors' names the same way each time. If you type Horst, J. S. for one entry and Horst, Jessica S. for another, the software will treat me as two different people. This can also happen for authors who do not consistently use their middle initial. What ends up happening is that you get first names in your in text references to differentiate these "people." If the problem is middle initials (i.e. you can't just change the name to match another entry), one solution is to tell the software to only display the publication year and then enter the names as a prefix (I often have to add a space at the end of prefixes and the beginning of suffixes).

You will also want to periodically check your references section to ensure there are not unwanted oddities (e.g. a line break because you accidentally have a blank line in a title; the doi URL at the start of the doi field).

Don't lose track: track changes

Sometimes when you are writing you just want to try something out, but you don't want to necessarily destroy the original. Or sometimes you need to cut words but there are some you might want to cut as a last resort. In situations such as these a great tool is track changes (it's literally listed as "track changes" in the tools in Microsoft Word, also under "reviewing").

When you turn on track changes Word will start color-coding changes you make. When you add new text, it will underline as you write. When you delete text, it will either strike through (~~like this~~, on a PC) or add a bubble in the margin (Mac), which allows you to still see what was written if you want to un-delete the text. There are buttons to accept or reject changes.

Tracking changes is helpful when you are writing alone because you can compare earlier versions without having multiple files and without having to remember which draft had the earlier version. I find it especially helpful when I need to cut words to reach a low word count: I track what I delete or change, and then if I cut enough words, I can put things back in if I liked them better than the new edits.

When working as part of a team, track changes is arguably even more helpful: you can track your own changes, show someone else how you've updated the text or follow along as someone else edits. The computer will color-code who made which changes, but this color-coding will change each time you close and reopen the file. As a student I found it very helpful when I would give my mentors drafts to read and they would use track changes to change the wording or move things around. Now, as a nonstudent I find it really helpful when I'm working with collaborators to see when and where text has been added and still how my own writing can be improved. There is a button to accept all changes in a document. If you receive a draft back from a supervisor with lots of changes it can be very tempting to just click that one button, but I'm certain that you will ultimately become a better writer if you go through each change item by item and accept as you read.

> "Tracking on Word is amazing! I am now an editing queen! I use this a lot when asked to overlook a letter, essay, etc., but definitely wish I had known how to use it prior to my project."
>
> —Naureen, BSc
> Education Center Manager

Here is another warning if your faculty mentor uses track changes: seeing lots of changes is normal – especially on a PC because all of the new text will be highlighted *and* all of the deleted text will be not-black too. For example, consider what happens when you simply change the following:

Recent research by Fake and colleagues (2014) shows that track changes improves the productivity of workers.
to
Recent research ~~by Fake and colleagues (2014)~~ shows that track changes improves *workers'* ~~the~~ productivity ~~of workers~~ (Fake et al., 2014).

It will show thirteen words changed (with only sixteen in the original that can feel like a lot!) even though the only changes are moving the reference to the end and changing "the productivity of workers" to "workers' productivity."

I still remember the elation I felt when I got a draft back from my own mentor that included a full sentence that had no changes – just keep at it. One more warning: try not to be annoyed if things get changed back in later versions. Sometimes a document evolves and what didn't work for version 1 might now work well for version 4.

No comment?

Similar to the use of track changes is the use of comments. In both Word and Excel you can add comments to your files. (I actually don't like this in Excel, but many people do.)

In Word, you highlight some text, click the "add comment" button and you'll get a bubble in the margin to type into. Later, you can see if there is a comment because the text will be highlighted a color to match the comment or there will be another sign. In Excel, you click on a cell, click the "add comment" button and a note field like a bubble will come up. Later, you can see if there is a comment because there will be a red triangle in the top right corner of the cell.

Comments are handy when you are working alone because you can add notes to yourself without messing up your word count. For example, in the Word document that I'm currently typing in, if I scroll up to where I wrote "I frequently write with typos (like teh)." I have a comment on the word "teh" that says, "Watch this word, make sure it is spelled wrong on purpose!" Another thing I like about comments is that it's easy to see them, so I am unlikely to print something with a leftover comment I haven't deleted.

When working as part of a team, comments can also be a useful way to communicate, again without messing up the word count or flow of the document. For example, I've used comments with collaborators many times to highlight things like "need a reference here," "this is too wordy" and even "I like this part you added, it sounds really good."

There are some situations when you cannot place a comment exactly where you want to (e.g. in the caption of a figure), but you can easily comment nearby and note something like, "The figure caption needs to include. . . ." I have learned the hard way not to actually make comments over references (my previous reference software constantly crashed when I would do that), but again right before or after the references it is not difficult to add a comment like "also cite John's study" or whatever.

Box 4.2: Where was I again?

Sometimes when I'm writing I like to effectively bookmark where I am and then look at a different section of the document and then get back to where I was (it's not always the end when you have a references section or if you are editing a results section and have already written most of the discussion). My low-tech hack for this kind of situation is to insert a $ where I want to mark my place (£ would work too). I don't do research that involves money, so when I want to get back if I use the "find" function to get to $ only one result will show up (where I just was) – as opposed to if I had used another symbol like ! or %. As a precaution I could also search for $ before submitting or printing my document to ensure I deleted the $ when I did resume writing.

Color-code to mark your place

When you are checking or editing a document, a spreadsheet or a presentation you can color-code to keep your place. (I'm using the term *color-code* loosely because sometimes bold or underline can serve the same function.) Do not underestimate the energy savings of using color-coding in these situations. For example, if you have data for twenty-four participants entered into Excel, but you have to check the data was entered properly, you can either change the color of the cells with the participant ID numbers, make the ID numbers bold or a different font color. Then, as you go through, turn them back to regular as they are checked – if someone interrupts you, you will know exactly where you left off.

This can also be great for presentations. For example, if you know the slide background color you want to end up with, you can manually change the slide background color of any slides you need to edit or work on to something else (e.g. pale blue, gray) and change them to white (or your finished color) as you go. Then you don't need to wonder, "Did I list all the key points on this slide?" because your computer will give you a sign.

This kind of color-coding also works for writing documents. For example, I often base my article abstracts off of the first paragraph of my discussion sections (p. 141). When I do this, I will copy and paste the discussion paragraph to the abstract and change the font color. Then, as I edit the paragraph to make it more abstract-like I will change the font color for each line. It can also be helpful to highlight where you mention figures (e.g., "see Figure 1" or "As can be seen in Figure 2 . . .") so you can check the numbering is really in the right order before you submit.

Color-coding text can also be helpful if you are just inserting something as a note to yourself. For example, I actually wrote Chapter 6 before this one and had a line that read, "Don't make dashed lines too thin/tiny" in red font for several days to remind me not to forget to tell you about that. It was in red because it wasn't the final version of the sentence. Such color-coding makes it easy to check the final version for notes to yourself that you don't want other people to read – which is a good thing as even professionals have let some embarrassing notes slip through (e.g. there was a recent news splash about a published article that contained "should we cite that crappy [name] paper here?" but the name of the other author was actually printed!). I know several people who use this kind of color-coding as a reminder that they have to insert a reference. Some writers will just write something like {{REF}} and then use the find function to check if all the {{REF}}s are updated, but I think color-coding works better in case there is a typo. Of course, these methods are not mutually exclusive: you could type {{REF: crappy paper here}} in bold red with yellow highlight if you wanted to be extra cautious. (Also double-check every paper you cite is in the references list.)

Box 4.3: Have a way with Word: clever things Word can do for you

- **Insert a page break.** This is helpful if you have a paragraph with only two or three lines or a new section header (e.g. Results) that you would like to start on a fresh page.
- **Have a different header on the first page.** Useful if the first page is a cover page.
- **Start page numbers from a number greater than 1.** You can choose any number to start from. This can be helpful if you are making different sections in different document files but will print them out and combine into one file (e.g. if each chapter is its own file, but you want Chapter 2 to start on page 21 because Chapter 1 ended on page 20). (Look for the *format* button near where you insert page numbers). You can also choose Roman numerals (helpful for some documents).
- **Use Autocorrect to create shortcuts.** Instead of writing the same phrase repeatedly, use autocorrect to fill the phrase out for you.
- **Add headers and footers** (text that appears on each page). Use this feature if you need to include a running head or your name/ title on each page.
- **Password protect a document.** Look under the preferences for Word not the preferences for the file, even to protect just one file. You can also password protect Excel workbooks.
- **Merge documents.** Use this feature if you and someone else have both edited a file (or you accidentally edited two different versions) to get all of the changes into one new document, then continue from there.
- **Use "find" to catch your mistakes.** If you need to write a common word that has another common word typo (e.g. trial and trail; that and hat) use the find function before you print or send your document to check that your participants did not complete any "trails" in your study.

- **Change margin width or page length.** Word will let you change the space the text can fill from the default settings. Really ask yourself if you need this though. Sometimes it is helpful to be able to fit everything onto one page (e.g. for instructions or consent forms) but for formal documents you aren't fooling any one – your mentor probably learned this trick years ago!

Tip: You can combine PDFs

Sometimes it makes sense to merge several documents together. When some of these are Word files and some are PDFs, print/save the Word files to PDFs. Then, you can merge the PDFs. A quick Internet search of "combine PDFs" or "merge PDFs" will provide you with software options for this task.

Number crunching

I used to *hate* Excel. I thought it was so ugly. It wasn't until I started really using it that I realized its beauty. Now, I daresay it's my favorite program. After I learned I can change the font, font color, background color and even add lines for borders, Excel became much prettier to me.

I have completely embraced using formulas for entering data. Some common formulas are in Table 4.1. Having Excel do simple computations that I can do in my head seems unproductive to some (Foreshaw, 2013), but why should I bother adding up how many trials every single participant completed when I can put a formula in Excel once and then copy the formula? I have other more interesting things to think about, like which colors I want to use for my bar graph or even what I want to watch on TV later. Plus, if I'm honest: Excel is better at math than I am. If Excel sums the total number of trials completed (e.g., sum(D2:F2)) I have a lot of confidence that Excel will be accurate every time. If I do it myself, there is some chance I'll make a human calculation error eventually *and* there is some chance I'll have a typo, like typing 14 instead of 13. Finally, if there is a problem, it is often easier to figure out where the problem is if you have additional columns with formulas – it's like showing your work on an algebra problem. (If you don't want to see all of the columns all the time, keep in mind you can hide columns in Excel, see Box 4.4.).

TABLE 4.1

Basic Excel Formulas

Formula	Example	Notes
Count	count(B1:B12)	Counts the numbers of cells within a range (e.g. for cells B1 to B12) that have a value entered
Max	max(B1:B12)	Reports the largest number (e.g. for cells B1 to B12)
Mean	mean(B1:B12)	Reports the average (e.g. for cells B1 to B12)
Median	median(B1:B12)	Reports the median (e.g. for cells B1 to B12)
Min	min(B1:B12)	Reports the smallest number (e.g. for cells B1 to B12)
Mode	mode(B1:B12)	Reports the mode (e.g. for cells B1 to B12)
Sqrt	Sqrt(B13)	Reports the square root of a number. This can be combined with stdev to calculate standard error (stdev/sqrt(n)).
Stdev	stdev(B1:B12)	Reports the standard deviation (e.g. for cells B1 to B12)
Sum	sum(B1:B12)	Adds up values in a range (e.g. for cells B1 to B12)

Tip: Color-code formulas

If you find a problem in your data file you will want to know if it was a problem at the (human) data-entry stage or if you made a mistake in your formula. In order to easily determine if information in a cell was entered by hand or the result of a formula, I color-code my formulas by making the font grey in those cells. That alerts me to not touch those cells (Excel is doing the work for me) and if I think something is wrong I know to click on the cell and look at the formula bar to see if my formula was correct.

Sometimes the problem is simply that Excel was told to take information from the wrong place (maybe average(C2:G2) instead of average(D2:H2)). Often if you put your cursor on the cell numbers (e.g. C2) they will show up in another color and be outlined in the spreadsheet. You can also move the outline to adjust which cells are called in the formula.

At random

One way to randomize your stimuli or trial order is to type a list of your stimuli/trials in one column in Excel, then in the next column use the rand() function (see Table 4.2) and sort by the random numbers. However, you may want to copy and paste-special the values otherwise they are likely to change each time you hit return while your document is

TABLE 4.2

Intermediate Excel Formulas

Formula	Example	Notes
Binomdist	Binomdist (k,N,p,false)	Reports the binomial p value for "exactly k out of N with the probability of p."
Binomdist	Binomdist (k,N,p,true)	Reports the binomial p value for "at least k out of N with the probability of p."
Chidist	Chidist (Chi-value,df)	Reports the p value for a Chi-Square test value with given degrees of freedom
Concatenate	Concatenate (B1,C1)	Merges information from cells together (e.g. if B1 is "male" and C1 is "Control" concatenate(B1,C1) will report "maleControl"). It is possible to add other information (e.g. concatenate(B1," ",C1,"_ group") would report "male Control_ group"). (This is also useful for combining first and last names.)
Correl	Correl (B1:B12,C1:C12)	Reports the correlation value for two ranges (e.g. cells B1 to B12 with cells C1 to C12).
Mid	mid (B1,4,10)	Reports the values for a given cell from one character/digit to another (e.g. if B1 is *newcontrol* mid(B1,4,10) will report *control* (the 4th character is c the 10th is l)).
Rand	Rand()	Reports a random number between 0 and 1
Rand between	Randbetween (1,100)	Reports a random number between two values (e.g. 1 and 100).
T.Test	T.Test (B1:B12,C1:C12,2,1)	Reports the p-value associated with a t-test (e.g. comparing cells B1 to B12 with cells C1 to C12). Note the third item (2 in the example) is the number of tails and the final item is the type of test (1 = paired, 2 = unpaired equal variances, 3 = unpaired, unequal variances).
Vlookup I	Vlookup ("M12",A1:B20,2)	Looks up vertically (v) to find a value or text in a range and reports the value that matches from another cell (e.g. looks for "M12" in A1 to A20 and reports the value in the second column (B) when it finds it). Note, use quotation marks for text, include all columns in the range and include the column number as the final number.
Vlookup II	Vlookup (40,A1:B20,2,false)	Same as vlookup I but adding false will make Excel only report back if it finds the exact value (e.g. 40) you specify.

open. Another method is to search online for a random number-generator tool. Often these will allow you to choose if you want to sample the random numbers with or without replacement.

Another method is to use a Latin Square or list every possible order (e.g. ABC, ACB, BAC, BCA, CAB, CBA) and then replace the place holders (e.g. A) with your actual stimuli.

What if . . .

My favorite Excel formula is "if." There are, in fact, a whole family of Excel formulas that include "if." These special formulas can do some standard things but also evaluate data *before* carrying out certain evaluations.

The standard if formula is if(something is true, then do this, else do that). For example, if(B13>5,B13+10,0) means if the value in B13 is greater than 5, then report B13 plus 10, but if it's not (else, otherwise) report 0. You can use this formula to also report back words, like if(B13>5,"too high", "normal range"). You can add if to many other functions as well (see Table 4.3).

TABLE 4.3

Excel Formulas Using If Functions

Formula	Example	Notes
If…Then	If (B13=12,"ok", "ERROR")	Completes an operation based on a contingency: if this, then, else (e.g. if the value in cell B13 is 12, then report "ok," if not (else/otherwise) report "ERROR")
Countif	countif (B1:B12, "male")	Counts the numbers of cells within a range (e.g. for cells B1 to B12) that have a specific value such as "male" or "100%."
Sumif I	Sumif (B1:B12,">0")	Sums a range if *those cells* match a criterion (e.g. sums B1 to B12 but only for values greater than zero). When using text or mathematical symbols use quotation marks.
Sumif II	Sumif (B1:B12, "male", C1:C12)	Sums a range if *another range* matches a criterion (e.g. sums C1 to C12 if the corresponding cells in B1 to B12 display "male"). Note the range you are summing is the second range.
Averageif I	Averageif (B1:B12,">0")	Averages a range if *those cells* match a criterion (e.g. averages B1 to B12 but only for values greater than zero). When using text or mathematical symbols use quotation marks.
Averageif II	Averageif (B1:B12, "male", C1:C12)	Averages a range if *another range* matches a criterion (e.g. averages C1 to C12 if the corresponding cells in B1 to B12 display "male"). Note the range you are averaging is the second range.

Sort yourself out

Excel can sort your data for you. You can enter your data as it comes in and then tell Excel to "sort by" the column that includes *condition* and "then by" the column that includes *sex*. This makes it easier to calculate means for each condition. However, be sure to *highlight the rows you want to sort from the row numbers*. If you do not highlight the entire row across, Excel will *only* sort what you did highlight. For example, if your data spans columns A to G and you accidentally only highlight A to D, then that will be sorted by will not match up with E–G. This can have enormous serious consequences because there may not be anything in the data to alert you to the fact that the data in row 3 is not all from the same participant. Sadly, I learned this lesson myself the hard way.

Tip: Variable names and stimuli names

Use real names not coded variables like 1 and 2. Before you analyze your data you can always go back and find and replace to make "experimental group" 1 and "control group" 2. Using real words helps avoid mistakes (it's not difficult to hit the 2 key when you mean the 1 key, but how likely is it you will type eontrol group (and if you did you would probably notice)? An added bonus is that if you meet with someone else about your data, you don't need to spend time answering, "Is the control group condition 1 or 2?" or "What is condition 1 again?"

Excel will try to anticipate what you want to type based on what was entered before in the same column. This can be annoying when you have multiple options that start with the same letter (e.g. pre-test, post-test), so you may want to name items carefully in Excel to speed up data entry (e.g. before and after instead of pre- and post-test, though I'd recommend using the more formal pre- and post-test in your paper). Some common letter substitutions are R for Thursday and U for Sunday (because T and S are already taken by Tuesday and Saturday, respectively).

See the errors of your ways

A lot of the columns in my data files exist to check my work. I cannot tell you how terrible it feels to analyze data and see a beautiful p value that is less than .05, only to then realize there was some typo and after fixing the typo discover that the beautiful p value was just an illusion. I don't want you to have to go through that heartache.

Tip: Be case sensitive

Many software programs are highly case sensitive and will treat things like Control group and control group as two different groups. This can obviously be problematic. Decide how or whether you will use capital letters and then be forever consistent with that decision.

Check individual scores

It is possible to have an incorrect score entered for a participant (e.g. typing 11 instead of 1). One way to check for this is to insert a column that sums the information before it (e.g. sum(B2:D2)). You can also insert another column that evaluates that total so you don't have to. For example if(E2>3,"CHECK!","OK"), that is if the value in E2 is greater than 3, display CHECK but otherwise display OK. You can also have Excel simply count how many values you have entered in a range (e.g. count(B2:D2)).

If you had categorical responses, you could do something like use the countif formula to count how many times you had each possible response, then add those sub-columns up to ensure they totaled the correct number of trials.

Check for outliers

Below your columns you can initially check for outliers caused by typos by using the min and max formulas to ensure your smallest and largest scores are within the correct range. Or you can use countif to check that there are no scores above or below a certain cut-off, for example countif(D2:D21,">10").

You can also calculate your mean and standard deviation (see Table 4.1) to determine if any scores are greater or less than the mean plus 2SD. For example average(D2:D21)+2*(stdev(D2:D21)) and average(D2:D21)-2*(stdev(D2:D21)). Then you can use countif to determine if any values in the original range are larger than those values (type the results of those values into your countif formula).

Check for human (reading) error

Now, those checking methods are helpful to check for typos that are unusual, but what about if you enter the wrong number and the wrong number is still realistic (like misspelling with a word spell check will still accept)? I know several labs that pair students up and have one experimenter enter the data and then the second experimenter takes the hardcopies and follows along with what is entered and checks it. This is OK, but it is really boring and I've noticed when I'm the second person checking I zone out without realizing it (like when you're reading a textbook and suddenly realize your eyes have been moving but you haven't actually been reading).

My solution is to set up the original data entry sheet, then "copy worksheet." One experimenter enters the data on the original sheet and the second one on the second sheet. But the data obviously won't be the same unless the participants are entered in the same order, so in the participant ID column I tell the second sheet to display what is in that cell on the original sheet. Simply click on a cell you want to be the same, type = and then click on the cell you want it to duplicate – even if it's on another page. Finally, I create a third worksheet and use that to check the other sheets are the same. For cell A1, I start typing my if-then formula, =if(, then I click on cell A1 in the first sheet, type = and click on cell A2 in the second sheet, then I continue my formula and tell Excel to display nothing (space) if they are identical or ERROR! if they are not. The formula will look something like:

=if(Sheet1!A1=Sheet2!A1,"","ERROR!")

Then, I copy that for all of the rows and columns.

Graph as you go

For ethical reasons, you should set your sample size based on your expected effect sizes and then test participants until you reach that sample size (and then not continue) and you should not keep testing until you like the data and then stop (a.k.a. p-hacking). However, there are still times when you may want to have an idea of what the data kind of look like as you are entering your data – this can be a useful transferable skill if you later work in sales or need to keep track of some other kind of data.

In these cases you may want to graph as you go. If you have straightforward scores that you are entering manually, having blank (un-entered) scores will be no problem and you will still get an average. However, if you are using formulas to sum your scores, Excel will (correctly) display 0 for un-entered scores. If you had 10 scores entered and 10 not entered, your mean would be very far off because Excel would be including 10 zeros to calculate that average. In this case, you might want to use average if and tell Excel to only average scores that are greater than 0.

> ### Tip: Get ready to graph
>
> *I like to include a separate worksheet where I put all of the means and standard errors that will go into my graph, then graph from there. On that sheet I simply create my 2×2 table (or whatever size for my design) and to get the values for the cells in that table I just type = and click on the cell from whatever worksheet has the information I need. I make an identical table below and instead of the means I link to the standard errors. This makes adding error bars easier because standard error rows and columns are in the same order as the means.*

Copy with care

In Word and other programs, when you copy and paste something it will paste a copy of the original in the new location. Excel will do this too, but it can also do something much more powerful – or problematic, if you don't know how it works.

If you have a formula in a cell and copy and paste that cell, Excel will paste the formula, not the value. For example, imagine you have pre-test scores in column B and the average (71) in cell B13 and that cell B13 is using the formula average(B1:B12). If you copy and paste B13 to C13 it will not copy over 71. Instead, Excel will copy and update the formula to average(C1:C12). Similarly, if you copy and paste to B14, Excel will copy and update the formula to average(B2:B13). This can actually be extremely useful if you will be using the same formula again (e.g. if column C had post-test scores).

If you really want to copy the value and not the formula you can tell Excel, but you have to do this manually (Excel defaults to thinking that you want to copy formulas). You can do this by choosing "paste special: values" instead of just regular paste.

Now, sometimes you want to always have Excel link to a specific cell, row or column (e.g. if you are dividing a lot of numbers by your sample size or making a chi-square table by hand). Insert a $ before the number (row) or letter (column) that you want to hold constant. For example:

- If you used the formula sum($A$1:$A$12) you would get the sum of cells A1 to A12 no matter where you put that formula, no matter how many times you copy and pasted it because both the column ($A) and the rows ($1,$12) are constant.

- If you used the formula sum($A1:$A12) and copy and pasted it two columns to the right and two rows down, Excel would update to sum($A3:$A14): same column ($A) but different rows.
- If you used the formula sum(A$1:A$12) and copy and pasted it two columns to the right and two rows down, Excel would update to sum(C$1:C$12): same rows ($1,$12) but different column.

Replace with care

I use find and replace a lot with Excel. This is especially handy when you are doing something you have already done with just a small change. For example, imagine you used Excel to make your test sheets for a study that involved questions about movie celebrities and now you want to use the same general method but include questions about TV celebrities. Instead of re-creating everything from scratch, you could simply replace item by item.

Be very careful if you do this, though. For example, if you've typed 11 and then replace 1 with 5, Excel will change 11 to 55. More worryingly, if you have a formula like min(C2:C12) it will also replace the 1 in that: min(C2:C52).

Box 4.4: Excel with Excel: Clever things Excel can do for you

- **Copy and paste value, formulas or formatting** (under "paste special").
- **Freeze panes and windows.** For example, you can freeze column A so that as you scroll to the right column A is always visible. I use this feature in every data worksheet to ensure I am looking at the participant row I think I am looking at.
- **Add comments.** Handy if you want to make a note to yourself like, "This is the participant who left to use the men's room halfway through" but you don't want to take up a column for that note. You may need to remove comments before you can paste into another program like SPSS.
- **Color-code either font or cell.** You can change the font color like you can in Word and PowerPoint (sometimes I find it handy to have data from different conditions in different colors) but you can also change the cell background colors, which can be handy, for example, to highlight which cells are headers for different measures.

- **Hide information from yourself.** You can hide both columns and rows. When a row or column is hidden the numbers (rows) or letters (columns) next to the hidden information turn blue so you know there is something hidden. For example, if you hide column C, the B and D for the neighboring columns will be blue. If you need multiple columns to calculate a variable or you have information that you don't always need (perhaps age and sex) you can hide this information but still have access when you do need it.
- **Transpose.** Excel can flip columns and rows. For example, if you entered data as two columns and three rows, you can change this to three columns and two rows. Copy (not cut) the area you want flipped, then highlight another area that is the new size (these cannot overlap) and using right-click choose "transpose."
- **Randomize your stimuli or trials** by generating random numbers with rand() and randbetween(x,y).
- **Fit material to one printed page.** Under "page set-up" you can tell Excel to print so that everything fits on one page (it will keep shrinking the text until it fits).
- **Merge cells.** This allows you to have cells wider or taller than a single cell. This is helpful for situations like tables where you want a heading over several columns (e.g. row 1 could include "test trials" and row 2 could include titles for each test trial).
- **Change Alignment.** You can decide if you want the text at an angle (useful if you have long column names) or even centered vertically within cells.
- **Duplicate worksheets.** If you click on a tab and press Ctrl you can move or copy the sheet. This is handy if you want to make multiple test sheets for participants who are similar but not quite identical: make one, copy it, then make the changes.
- **Name your tabs.** Double-click on a tab to rename it. It is handy to label "raw data" versus "data for SPSS" or "quotes" versus "orders."

Pivot tables

Perhaps one of my favorite features of Excel is pivot tables. Pivot tables only work if your data are entered such that you have one row per *data point,* so you might have many rows for a single participant. This is especially useful if you have collected data with software such as ePrime.

If your data are entered like this, you can create a "pivot table report," which will open a new table where you can drag and drop items that you want for the rows (e.g. condition, participant ID) and the columns (e.g. trial type, trial number). You can have multiple row and column headings (e.g. you can sort by condition, then by participant). Then you drag and drop your scores (or reaction times) into the main body of the table. This will provide you with a great table where you can see all of your data at once. The default setting is to display the count (which is handy to ensure participants are contributing the correct number of data points) but you will likely want to change that to average. By double-clicking on a value that looks out of place, Excel can show you which information went into displaying that value. You can also filter your data by hiding different information such as blank scores.

Pivot tables are very, very powerful and useful in many (but not all) situations. If you are interested in using a pivot table, look for tutorials and walk-throughs online as pivot table settings change with each major version of Excel. Another lab member may also be able to sit down with you and show you how to use them. I learned everything I know about pivot tables from a mentor showing me how to create one and then spending time tinkering with them myself (lots of dragging and clicking).

Common Excel errors

Circular reference

If you get this error, look in the formula bar to ensure you are taking the values from the correct cells. Excel will alert you to this error if something can't be calculated because part of the answer requires the answer. It's kind of a chicken-and-egg or Catch22 situation. For example, imagine you have entered most of your data in rows 1 to 20 and your averages, standard deviations, etc., are reported in row 22. If you discover that the last participant's data needs to be excluded, let's say there was an experimenter error you need to check into, and you move that participant's row of data down past row 24 (e.g. perhaps to row 30) your formula for the average in column C might change from =average(C1:C20) to =average(C1:C30) but that range includes C22. Excel can't calculate the average of a series of numbers that includes itself, so it will tell you that you have a circular reference.

###

If you see this, make the relevant column wider. Cells will show only ### if the column width is too small for the entire number to fit.

#DIVX/0!

This error is simply that Excel is trying to divide a number by nothing or zero, which is not possible mathematically.

#NUM! and #VALUE!

Excel cannot compute something because it was expecting a number or value and you have entered something else in one of the cells it is trying to compute about.

A final note, it can often be faster and more ergonomic to use keyboard shortcuts rather than always reaching for your mouse. Table 4.4. lists some common keyboard shortcuts you should know.

TABLE 4.4

Common Keyboard Shortcuts

	PC Shortcut	Mac Shortcut	What It Does
Time Saving	Ctrl + z	Cmd + z	Undoes last action (you can press this multiple times); use y to revert back
	Ctrl + del	Cmd + del	Deletes text to the *right* of the cursor
	Ctrl + d *or* Ctrl + shift + f	Cmd + d *or* Cmd + shift + f	Opens a menu where you can change the font and also make your highlighted text ^{superscript}, $_{\text{subscript}}$, ~~struck through~~, SMALL CAPS, etc. Especially useful for formulas and things like η_p^2
	Ctrl + p	Cmd + p	Opens menu to print
	Ctrl + s	Cmd + s	Saves your file
	Ctrl + f	Cmd + f	Opens "find" function
	Ctrl + tab	Cmd + tab	Flip to another window (the last thing you accessed)
	Window m	Cmd + m	Minimizes window
Moving	Ctrl + a	Cmd + a	Selects "all" of your text.
	Ctrl + c	Cmd + c	Copies highlighted text (original will remain)
	Ctrl + x	Cmd + x	Cuts highlighted text (original will not remain)
	Ctrl + v	Cmd + v	Pastes copied/cut text to this location
Formatting	Ctrl + u	Cmd + u	Underlines; use i to italicize; use b to make bold
	Ctrl + l	Cmd + l	Aligns text to the left; use r to align to the right; use j to justify (align both left and right)
	Ctnl + shift + >	Cmd + shift + >	Increases the font size (you can press this multiple times); use < to decrease
	Ctrl + 2	Cmd + 2	Double-spaces your text (use 1 for single-spacing and 5 for 1.5 spacing)

Note: related shortcuts are noted in the right-hand column to keep the table brief.

Transferring these skills

Computers are supposed to be a tool, not the activity that you do. It's reasonable for a software engineer or the manager for a large automated production system to say, "I work with computers," but that probably won't be how you want to describe your next job – and yet it's likely to be true. There are very few jobs that do not require using a computer (even artists often sell their work using websites and maintain spreadsheets of their expenses and profits). My goal with this chapter was to give you insights into how you can use the computer as the tool it is meant to be so you can get on with the activity you are really doing (writing, number crunching, etc.). No matter what you do next, you won't want to spend an hour looking for a computer file because it was named *ABreport.docx* instead of something less obscure like *annual-budget-report.docx*.

I've tried to write this chapter as a quick reference guide you can refer back to when you start a new job. "Yes, I know how to use Excel" you might say in a job interview, but perhaps before the first day you want to refresh yourself with these key formulas. Your first week on the job, you might not want to run to your supervisor every time you get an error message in Excel: now that you've read this chapter you have an idea about how to correct some of the most common errors. Once you find yourself collaborating on writing projects (perhaps a new company mission statement) you can use track changes effectively. And if your annoying coworker was working on the same document at the same time you may recall that Word can cleverly merge the documents so you don't have to compare each paragraph manually to spot the differences.

References

Allen, D. (2001). *Getting Things Done: How to Achieve Stress-free Productivity.* London: Penguin Books.

Foreshaw, M. (2013). *Your Undergraduate Psychology Project.* Chichester, UK: British Psychological Society and John Wiley & Sons Ltd.

5 The write way

Before you continue reading this chapter, keep in mind that I won't be marking or grading your paper. If your faculty mentor gives you advice that is different from mine, follow your mentor's advice: he/she is the one who will grade your paper and knows the culture of your department! (But if the difference pertains to APA style, check the latest APA manual.)

Remember, this is not a book about writing or statistics (p. 1) – there are entire books devoted to those topics – including the APA manual, which I highly encourage you to use as your write your dissertation. This book is about skills you can use after you complete your research project – and clear written communication is one of those skills. So, although I will go over the structure of your dissertation and provide insight into the specific sections of your paper, my main goal remains helping you hone general skills like clear, concise writing that you can continue to use long after you have submitted your dissertation.

Your dissertation should look and feel like a professional journal article submission. When articles are submitted they aren't typeset in single-spaced columns, they are long double-spaced manuscripts, usually with all of the tables and figures at the end. This is the format faculty are used to reading when they review papers, and you want your paper to look and feel just like a paper they might be reviewing for an academic journal. But do check if there are special formatting requirements in your department (like there are for specific publishers).

So, how do you make your paper look and feel like a journal manuscript? Reading, mimicry and polishing. First, know that the more you read, the better you will write. When you read papers consider what works and what doesn't work. For example, if the results section is confusing ask yourself what the authors could have done to make it easier for you to read, or if the results section is easy to follow try to figure out what the authors did to make it so. These examples will show you what to do and what not to do.

Second, as you write, mimic the papers you found easy to read. Note, I'm definitely *not* saying you should copy the words (that's plagiarism, see Box 5.1), but pay attention to the style. For example, I discovered that I really liked papers with hypotheses phrased as if-then statements. If whatever idea is correct, then participants should behave like this. If that's wrong, then participants should do the opposite. Now, I often use if-then statements to explain my own hypotheses, but here is an elegant example from Rebecca Gómez and colleagues (2006, p. 671): "If time alone triggers change, infants who nap between familiarization and test and infants who do not nap would be expected to show the same pattern of effects. However, if sleep is a determining factor, then performance would be expected to differ between the two conditions."

Box 5.1: Plagiarism

Hopefully, you have heard of plagiarism. You may have heard about it so many times that you are sick of hearing about it. But please, bear with me!

Plagiarism is the failure to give full credit for an idea, intellectual property or wording (even one's own earlier wording, which is why you will see authors cite themselves). Plagiarism is so serious that it can end careers (an example is a director of the Toronto District School Board).

Most students know better than to copy and paste large sections of text and try to pass the text off as their own writing. But sometimes plagiarism can be subtle and unintentional. I most often find plagiarized work is similar to Example 5 in Table 5.1. Adding a reference is not enough. Aim to write like in Example 7.

Example 5 is such an easy trap that I recommend when taking notes on studies you read that you paraphrase what you read in your own words from the beginning so you do not accidentally forget that you have copied something verbatim (for a similar tip see Foreshaw, 2013).

Third, plan to write multiple drafts and incorporate feedback. Your mentor frequently reads and edits other people's writing either by giving feedback to coauthors or through participating in the peer-review process. He or she may have written several, perhaps dozens of journal articles or could even be a journal editor – so your mentor will know what works and what doesn't, what the conventional way of writing something is and where students "lose marks" on their dissertations. Listen to all of the feedback – and follow it! Your mentor is trying to help you and you don't want to waste his or her time.

TABLE 5.1

Examples of reworking a text excerpt and discussion of why it is plagiarism (or not)

Original Text	Hypothetical Dissertation		Plagiarism? Why/Why Not?
"Stories that open by revealing outcomes may lead readers to anticipate additional revelations at the end; in other words, readers do not expect a story to provide complete premature knowledge of its ending the way an external source might." Leavitt and Christenfeld, 2011, p. 1153.	1	Stories that open by revealing outcomes may lead readers to anticipate additional revelations at the end.	Yes	Verbatim (word for word) without quotation marks and no reference. It is not clear that this is Leavitt and Christenfeld's idea and not the student's own.
	2	Stories that open by revealing outcomes may lead readers to anticipate additional revelations at the end (Leavitt & Christenfeld, 2011).	Yes	Verbatim without quotation marks. Although there is a reference it is not clear that this is Leavitt and Christenfeld's text, not the student's.
	3	Readers do not expect a story to provide complete premature knowledge of its ending the way an external source might. Stories that open by revealing outcomes may lead readers to anticipate additional revelations at the end.	Yes	Verbatim without quotation marks. Although the sentences are not in the same order as the original, it is not clear that this is Leavitt and Christenfeld's text, not the student's.
	4	Stories that begin by revealing the end may lead readers to anticipate additional revelations at the ending.	Yes	Although a few minor words have been changed to synonyms, it is not clear that this is Leavitt and Christenfeld's idea and not the student's own.
	5	Stories that begin by revealing the end may lead readers to anticipate additional revelations at the ending (Leavitt & Christenfeld, 2011).	Yes	A reference has been included, so it clear this idea is from Leavitt and Christenfeld, but although a few minor words have been changed to synonyms, the text is too close to the original to be the student's own work. Only 19 per cent of the original was changed.

(Continued)

TABLE 5.1 (Continued)			
Original Text	*Hypothetical Dissertation*		*Plagiarism? Why/Why Not?*
	6	"Stories that open by revealing outcomes may lead readers to anticipate additional revelations at the end." (Leavitt & Christenfeld, 2011, p. 1153).	No	By using quotation marks and a reference with a page number for the quote, it is clear this is Leavitt and Christenfeld's idea and wording. Although not plagiarism, this is not ideal because we cannot assess the student's understanding of this idea.
	7	Readers may expect stories in which the ending is revealed early to provide additional revelations later (Leavitt & Christenfeld, 2011).	No	This is what we all want: the reference makes it clear that the idea is Leavitt and Christenfeld's, but the wording is the student's.

"Draft, draft, draft and re-draft – make sure you read over it, proofread and learn to be brutal: if it does not sound right cut it or change it."

—Tash, BSc
Senior Occupational Health Therapy Assistant

When you get feedback, time may be of the essence. You may only have a few weeks left before you have to submit your dissertation or your supervisor may be fitting in reading your draft among several additional pressing deadlines. Although it feels good to hear "this is a great paragraph" and "you explained this well here," what you really need is a list of things to fix or improve. It can be easy for supervisors to approach feedback as, "I need to help this student fix anything wrong" instead of "I need to look for both weaknesses and strengths." So, don't be discouraged if the feedback you get back is 95 per cent negative. This doesn't mean that you're a terrible writer. In fact, it is likely a sign that your supervisor sees potential for your dissertation to be very good and is trying to help you reach that potential.

Many faculty provide feedback by tracking changes. This is helpful because they can provide comments and also change words or move things around and you can follow along because it is all tracked. However, documents can quickly look like everything is changed. For example, if a fourteen-word sentence is moved, both the new location and the original location will be highlighted, looking like twenty-eight words were changed when it was a simple re-location. If it looks like everything was changed don't panic: it's normal. I still remember a proud moment when I finally got a draft back from my PhD advisor in which a whole paragraph had remained unchanged from my original – and this didn't happen until *years* after I had completed my undergraduate research project.

Tip: Formatting for your mentor and supervisor

You may be writing your paper in single-spaced Calibri font size 11 so that you can see a lot of the text on the screen at once, but be sure to double-space your text and use the font you plan to use for the submission (e.g. Times New Roman 12). This will make your paper more like what your mentor is used to reading and enable him/her to get a better sense for how long each section really is. Plus, it will save you time and headache later because it will make the comments (either through track-changes or on a hardcopy) easier to read.

The sections of your dissertation

Your paper should have a lot in common with a feel-good summer blockbuster movie: it should be predictable, the audience should have a sense of where you are headed and the ending should wrap everything up nicely. To achieve this there is a set structure psychologists agree on: the hourglass (Bem, 1987). I depict this hourglass in Figure 5.1. This especially pertains to the introduction and discussion, so I return it to it below (p. 120).

There are many commonalities between journal articles/dissertations and movies: both tell a story, there are some aspects that are "formulaic" and there is a long time between when the footage is shot/the data is collected and the end product enters the public domain. Just like actors, authors are frequently remembered for masterpieces (and sometimes flops) but people also ask themselves questions like, "What has she done lately?"

Like movies, which are not necessarily shot in sequence, journal articles are also not necessarily written in sequence (i.e. the order in which

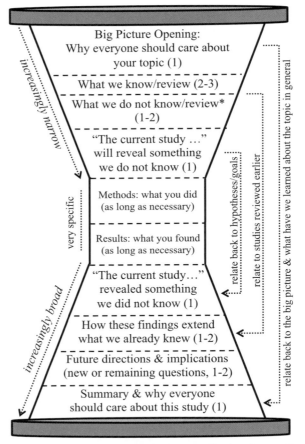

Figure 5.1 The hourglass structure of an academic paper. Numbers in parentheses/brackets indicate approximate numbers of paragraphs devoted to each topic.

they are read). Specifically, most researchers write articles in this order: method, results, introduction, discussion, abstract. This order is preferred because you can generally start writing the method section as soon as you are collecting data – after all, you would not be running your study properly if the method were changing! Once your data are collected, you can begin analyzing your results. It is much easier to write the introduction after you know what the results are (though you will want to be making notes to yourself as ideas come to you, see also lab notebook, p. 24). You will want to set your introduction up so that it predicts your results. Finally, once the introduction is written you can begin your discussion section.

Box 5.2: Formatting

Unless your department has other rules, format your paper like a journal article. Follow the latest APA manual, but here is the general idea:

- Include a title page with your title centered about one-third of the way down, following by your name (centered) and university (centered). On the top left write RUNNING HEAD: (in caps) followed by a short running head (e.g. the first five words of your title) also in caps.
- Put your abstract on page 2, with the heading Abstract centered.
- Start your paper on page 3, with the heading that is identical to your title. You do not need the word "Introduction."
- Double space everything. Not 1.5 space, but real double space.
- Use a traditional font like Times New Roman or Arial, even if that is not the default on your computer.
- Left justify the main text except for major headings, which should be centered. So, except for major headings (e.g. Method, Results) the main text should line up on the left and be "zig-zaggy" on the right. I know it's not as pretty as both left-and-right-justified – I don't make the rules.
- Add a header to the top right of each page. Put your running head (without the words "running head") and the page number. Right justify this.
- Include an Acknowledgements section, and thank your mentors and supervisors and anyone else who helped out.
- For figures and tables see Chapter 6.

Method

The method section should be written such that anyone else can read your paper and replicate what you did. Of course, not all authors write clearly enough or include enough detail for this to be possible, but this is the goal you should aim for. Your reader will take some things for granted, but in your first draft spell everything out and assume your reader needs a lot of details. It is *much* easier to cut information later than add more detail in – especially when you are dealing with a strict word limit!

The method section is quite formulaic, which makes it a good (read: easy) section to write early as you are honing your ability to write clearly and concisely. Because it is formulaic, often you can look to a paper with a similar method as a kind of template.

The method section includes paragraphs about the participants, stimuli, design and procedure. I often recommend collapsing design and procedure into one sub-section because the line between the two is often blurry. For example, it is difficult to write about how trials were administered without noting how many trials were administered and what the differences were between conditions.

Box 5.3: Why care about APA style

Did you know that the rock group Van Halen put in its concert contract that there should be a bowl of M&Ms in the dressing room without any brown Ms? This wasn't just a crazy celebrity behavior: it was a test. The band knew that if there wasn't a bowl, or if it included brown Ms, that the contract was not read closely. This could mean other more important things like equipment set-up was also not properly followed (which could be a major safety concern!) and should suggest that they cancel the show.

When I think of APA style, I think of Van Halen. If a student doesn't bother putting p in italics or formatting the references properly, how do I know that the other more important stuff (like proper informed consent procedures, debriefing, counterbalancing and experimental procedures) were followed? Following APA style isn't just busywork: it demonstrates that you take everything about the experiment seriously and pay attention to subtle details, which can sometimes make a big difference.

Results

Your results section should provide the results from your study in both statistical evidence and plain English. Each time you present a finding, repeat what it means in plain English and tie it back to your hypotheses (always present the statistics before the plain English recap, Harris, 2001). Be as precise as possible, and include which direction the result is in (i.e. which of the groups did better, not just that there was a difference between groups). Note, it is not the "result" that is significant, but the "association" or the "difference" between conditions (Foreshaw, 2013).

If you must complete preliminary analyses, put these in the first paragraph to get them out of the way. Preliminary analyses will include anything you do *not* want to be different between groups that could have influenced your results (e.g. age, vocabulary level, education, number of training trials needed to reach some criterion, length of time needed to complete the main task, number of hours participants sleep at night).

They may also include things you *do* want to have been different between groups before you started your study (e.g. typing speed if you want to compare proficient and novice typists, Bem, 1987).

Next, present your most impressive significant finding. What does "impressive" mean? Think of it in terms of difficult to obtain by chance. For example, if you run an ANOVA and find a significant 2×2 interaction, start with that and then mention the main effects. If you don't have a significant interaction but you do have a main effect start with that. Save all of your nonsignificant effects for the end of the paragraph – unless you only have nonsignificant effects, which happens but can also be informative.

If your results section is going to be long, consider including subheadings, but name these after what you measured or the aspect of the procedure they address and not the statistical test. That is, your headings should have names like *response times* and *error rates* not *ANOVA* and *Linear Regression*.

If your study involves comparing something against a chance level of responding, I recommend putting this information before any other analyses, such as comparisons between conditions. It is good to first establish that any change or learning even occurred before examining whether there is a difference between groups. There can be a difference between groups with everyone still not performing better than expected by chance (Horst, 2015).

If you have conducted a t-test and the results are significant at both one and two tails, report the two-tailed result. It is likely that you really do have an idea of which direction your results should go, but it is harder to get a significant p-value with two tails than with one, so the two-tailed test is considered more conservative (being conservative is a good thing in the world of psychology statistics). The .05 p-value you are hoping for corresponds to the 5 per cent at the end of the bell-curve/normal distribution. For a one-tailed t-test the entire 5 per cent is at one end of the curve, so you will reject the null hypothesis if your t-value is over approximately 1.64. In contrast, in a two-tailed t-test that 5 per cent is split among both ends of the curve, so you really have only 2.5 per cent at the ends. In this case you will reject the null hypothesis if your t-value is over approximately 1.96. Using a two-tailed test is like saying, "I'm not using alpha = .05, but the more conservative alpha = .025."

Introduction

Good introductions share a similar structure: they begin with a broad opening that makes the topic relevant and interesting for the reader. For example:

- "Mental illness is increasing in Canada globally with depression classified as the leading cause of disability worldwide (World Health Organization 2012)" (Krameddine, DeMarco, Hassel, & Silverstone, 2013, p. 1).
- "Moving the self in relation to other objects is a central problem faced by children and adults alike. We cross traffic-filled roads, walk along crowded sidewalks, and catch fast-moving balls" (Plumert, Kearney, & Cremer, 2007, p. 255).
- "Attention processes are vital to effective functioning in everyday life and for an individual's academic and general achievement" (Breckenridge, Braddick, & Atkinson, 2013, p. 271).

This is especially useful for student dissertations because you may not have much control over who is reading your dissertation. Your reader(s) could be from a very different area of psychology and might not care about depression, attention, language or whatever your topic is.

In the first paragraph you want to explain why *everyone* should care about your topic. You may want to include information about how what you are studying influences behavior in daily life or many situations that humans encounter or a problem that has large economic consequences.

In the subsequent paragraphs you will want to review the literature, but you will not necessarily review all of the literature that exists because you want to keep the hourglass structure and avoid plot holes (see Box 5.5).

Like in a movie, you also want to foreshadow where you are going and also provide information that would severely disrupt the flow later. Consider *Home Alone* (Columbus, 1990). In one early scene Kevin shoots action figures down the laundry chute to establish that there is a laundry chute from the kitchen to the basement. Toward the end of the movie, the laundry chute becomes important during the attempted burglary, but it would severely disrupt the flow to demonstrate its location. If there are key studies, such as complex theories that you will want to refer back to towards the end, you may want to introduce them in the beginning.

You want to set up the big picture, then what we know and after that what we don't know. Ideally, you want the reader to predict your study. You want the reader to start thinking, "I can't believe no one has put this together before. Someone should really do a study on ____." Then you swoop in with, "The current study examines ____." (People like being right so this can get your reader in a good mood too.)

> "Go back through dissertation and make sure every sentence adds something and that the introduction tells a story getting more specific as you read on."
>
> —Kerri, BSc
> Mental Health Recovery Worker

You only want to review studies that will help the reader predict what your study will be on, note issues you control for and issues that remain unanswered in the current literature – which you are going to answer with your study. If there are issues you are not going to answer they either belong in the discussion under "future directions" or they are deleted scenes (see Box 5.5).

Box 5.4: Plot holes and deleted scenes

Like a summer blockbuster, each "scene" (paragraph) in your paper should advance the plot. You should not have any unnecessary information, especially "plot holes." For example, if your paper is about men and women's feelings about the gender pay gap and you have an entire paragraph on gender differences in housework including that men are happier when they do more housework (Scott & Plagnol, 2012), this could be problematic. First, it might make your reader start predicting that your study was on something it wasn't (e.g. how pay divide influences housework divide or what happens in homes where the woman is has a larger salary), which could lead the reader to be resentful that you wasted their valuable reading time or frustrated that your study was only restricted to its narrow topic. Neither of these are feelings you want to evoke in your reader. Second, if this topic is not revisited later in the discussion it creates a plot hole your reader will want filled. Why did the author spend a paragraph on housework and not return to it? How does housework relate to the results and conclusions of the current study?

Because you want to avoid plot holes, you must learn to be OK with "deleted scenes" – paragraphs that may be beautifully written and interesting but that just aren't necessary to keep to advance the plot. It can be really difficult to delete good writing, but it is worth it for a good final product. I actually recommend that you create a separate file to paste your "deleted scenes" into in case you can use them someday for something else.

Discussion

As you can see in Figure 5.1, the Discussion is almost the mirror image of the Introduction. You will begin by restating the goals. This is almost the reverse of what you did with your "current study" paragraph at the end of the introduction. In real life, I frequently take my "current study" paragraph and use that as the basis for the opening paragraph in my Discussion. Remind the reader what the goals were and what you found.

Next, you want to relate your study back to other studies in the literature. You will generally be referring to studies you already described in the Introduction; for example if there was a study that had a confound you corrected in your study, you will likely note your study extends the previous study. Similarly, if there are two conflicting theories in the literature you will explain how your study provides evidence for one or the other (or not).

Although it is helpful to be consistent and refer back to the same studies cited in the Introduction, it is possible to bring in new information in the Discussion – if you can get the reader up to speed quickly. Consider *Home Alone* (Columbus, 1990) again. Unlike the gag with laundry chute, we see Kevin set the heating coil on the front door knob toward the end. This is a simple, easy-to-understand hazard so it is quick to explain at the end and needs no foreshadowing. In the non-Hollywood world of journal articles an equivalent might be references to similar results with another population or in a related task. Sometimes relating your study to one or more studies in the literature only makes sense after you have revealed your results. If something is vitally important to the interpretation of your findings (e.g. a theoretical perspective), however, you will want to mention it both in the introduction and in the end.

Towards the end of your Discussion you will want to add one to two paragraphs on "future directions" and/or "limitations." Future direction are useful because they allow you to demonstrate your creative and critical thinking as well as your understanding of how your data may be informative for others, sometimes including other areas of psychology.

Personally, I dislike reading limitations in student dissertations because we rarely have limitations in our published articles in my subfield. The assumption is that you designed your study very well and therefore there are not large limitations. (Noting a small sample size is always an odd limitation because it makes the reader wonder if the author didn't work hard enough to recruit participants or ran out of time.) However, check with your faculty mentor to see what he or she prefers and the norm for your subfield.

You can often spin a limitation as a possible future direction. For example if there is evidence to suggest you would find different results in a different version of the task or in a different population, then mention that future directions could involve that task or population.

Finally, include a final paragraph where you give concluding remarks and bring your readers back out to the big picture, reminding them why everyone should care about this topic. Ideally, come full circle (like how Kevin sees his neighbor though the window at the end of the movie, as he had done in an early scene, but now so much more is known, Columbus, 1990).

Tip: Size doesn't matter

A common limitation noted by students is sample size. This comes across as highly sophomoric. Almost any study could lead to a significant result if a large enough sample were tested (Field & Hole, 2003; Harris, 2001). Therefore, blaming sample size indicates only a very basic understanding of statistical power. Depending on your design, including the number of conditions, trials, data points and expected effect sizes, you may not need a very large sample size, so this becomes more of an issue of poor experimental design or inability to recruit sufficient numbers of participants (see also Foreshaw, 2013).

Abstract

Because the abstract covers everything (introduction, method, results, discussion) I find it especially useful to write it last, a bit like how movie trailers are created after the movie is in post-production. Often I will take the first paragraph of the discussion and use that to create the abstract. The abstract should start with a brief (one-sentence) introduction to the topic, then continue to what you did, how you did you it and what you found. Ideally, you want to conclude with by noting key implications.

> "Giving yourself enough time at the end to review it all and re-read it is really important. There are always little errors!"
> —Anna, BSc
> English as a Second Language Teacher

Title

Take a moment to think about some of the most memorable papers you've read recently (try to think of about four papers).

Hopefully, the papers that came to mind were each memorable because they had really strong data and very well-designed and controlled methods and were nice to read (not too dry or jargony). But in an ideal world every published paper would have great data and great methods and would be a pleasure to read. There are a lot of papers to keep track of, and I've noticed that the ones I personally can remember best tend to also have catchy titles. This is especially true for authors who have published many papers in the same area. For example, one of my mentors, Lisa Oakes, has published dozens of papers on infant categorization, but a few stand out for me with titles like "By land or by sea . . ." (in which infants saw land or sea animals, Oakes, Coppage, & Dingel, 1997), "hold your horses . . ." (in which infants held and played with toy horses and dogs, Kovack-Lesh & Oakes, 2007) and "the cat is out of the bag . . ." (in which infants looked at pictures of cats and some dogs – actually that title was my idea, Kovack-Lesh, Horst, & Oakes, 2008).

People reading your dissertation (e.g. second-markers/thesis committee members) may also be reading several other dissertations. One way to help make your paper highly memorable for these readers (besides having strong method and being a pleasure to read, of course!) is to have a catchy title. A few years ago, my masters student Emilly titled her dissertation "Crossing the line . . ." because her study involved children crossing a line on the floor when they were not supposed to. Recently, I was talking to a colleague about the study and he stopped me and asked, "Wait, is this the 'crossing the line' project?" He had clearly remembered it – more than three years later.

Clearly, I like "catchy titles," but some people don't. For example, the writers of the show *Seinfeld* were explicitly told not to spend their creative juices coming up with catchy titles for the episodes because the producers wanted them to focus on the actual writing. Ideally, you will choose your title as one of your last steps (see To-Do List, Chapter 1, p. 21) or you will choose your title as part of a productive break (see Chapter 3, p. 79). However, be sure to run your title by your mentor to double-check that a catchy title will go over well.

How do you create a catchy title? Here's my approach: I think of a word from the method I'm using (e.g. "cat") and then I go online and search for idioms with that keyword. Sometimes I use an online idiom dictionary. For some papers I fail to find anything useful so I move on to another word or just stick with a "boring" title.

Usually there is a list of a few alternatives to pick from (e.g. it's raining cats and dogs, look like something the cat brought in, the cat is out of the bag). I often look up the meaning of the idiom to make sure it fits and that there isn't a meaning I'm unfamiliar with. Then, I'll couple the idiom to something more specific (e.g. *The Cat is out of the Bag: The Joint Influence of Previous Experience and Looking Behavior on Infant Categorization*). Do watch out that you don't make your title so catchy that the reader cannot tell what the study is about!

Box 5.5: Examples of catchy titles

- Raeding Wrods With Jubmled Lettres: There Is a Cost (Rayner, White, Johnson, & Liversedge, 2006).
- What part of *no* do children not understand? A usage-based account of multiword negation (Cameron-Faulkner, Lieven, & Theakston, 2007).
- The pen is mightier than the keyboard: Advantages of longhand over laptop note taking (Mueller & Oppenheimer, 2014).
- Interfering neighbours: the impact of novel word learning on the identification of visually similar words (Bowers, Davis, & Hanley, 2005).
- For better and for worse: Genes and parenting interact to predict future behavior in romantic relationships (Masarik et al., 2014).
- The magical number seven, plus or minus two: some limits on our capacity for processing information (Miller, 1956).
- To thine own self be true: Psychological adjustment promotes judgeability via personality-behavior congruence (Human, Biesanz, Finseth, Pierce, & Le, 2014).

Avoid asking an unanswered question in your title. You want the reader to have a sense of what your findings are. A title such as *Does Social Media Use Increase Tendency to Gossip?* Is not as informative as *Social Animals: Media Use Increases Gossip*.

References

Completing your references section is tedious, but it is not technically difficult. Refer to the latest edition of the *American Psychological Association Publication Manual* for how to properly cite articles, chapters, books, etc. You can also look at the references sections from very recent articles (e.g. those published in the last year) for example formatting (but see also Box 4.1, p. 92).

When you read a paper and it cites another paper that you really want to cite yourself, be sure to track down that original paper and at least skim it (ideally, read it fully). It is possible that the authors of the more recent paper are misrepresenting the original or have their facts wrong or they could be citing the wrong paper. These things do happen. You want to double-check that what you write is accurate. In addition, writing something like, "Because there is no connection to a wider external world, language symbols do not have real meaning in artificial intelligence (Harnad, 1990 cited by Pezzulo et al., 2011)" looks lazy and implies you ran out of time to track down the original reference (for a lengthier discussion see Field & Hole, 2003).

> "It is SO important to fully reference as you go along . . . I fell in to the trap of only jotting down just book/article titles so I didn't 'lose my flow' whilst writing, assuming it wouldn't take long to go back to them at the end. Well it was one of the most time-consuming parts of the whole project and something I would never do again!"
> —Megan, BSc
> Operations Manager in Marketing co.

Appendices

Use appendices with caution. Only include one (or more) if you absolutely must. Do not include anything vital for understanding your paper – that material must be in the paper. Use the Appendix for additional materials that would be far too detailed for the actual paper, such as full verbatim instructions given to the participants, text participants were asked to read, questions on the questionnaire, special control analyses (but note general take-home messages of those findings in the results section), etc. (for more information see Harris, 2001).

How to write well

Writing is a highly transferable skill, whether you are writing materials for your prospective clients, training documents for your coworkers, or simply sending emails to your colleagues. It's true that you may not need APA style again (but see Box 5.4), but a lot of the tips and tricks to writing well in psychology apply to general writing as well. In fact, many of the APA style guidelines are also conventional grammar rules.

Repeat, repeat, repeat

Writing in psychology is very different from writing in the humanities. Beautiful psychology writing – yes, there is such a thing! – often includes a lot of *word repetition* because the terms mean very specific things. For example, in a philosophical essay, a writer might not want to appear to use a limited vocabulary and therefore have a sentence about *attention* followed by a sentence about *focus*. But in psychology, a writer is more likely to (correctly) repeat the word *attention* in every sentence because *attention* and *focus* may not mean the exact same thing – and because the reader might otherwise question, "Why did she write *focus*? How is that different from *attention*? There must be a reason she is using a new term . . ." (for a similar argument see Bem, 1987). Repeating your words can be a difficult habit to adopt, especially if you have experience writing in the non-sciences. Until you master repeating your words you may need to read your drafts closely to look for synonyms.

Of course, there are times when you do not want to repeat words, but this applies mainly to adjectives (e.g. "a critical distinction among these important studies" sounds better than "an important distinction among these important studies"). When it comes to concepts and jargon: repeat yourself.

Only move forward

You want each paragraph to advance the story you are telling. You do not want to discuss one topic, a second topic and then return to the first topic. Sometimes I find this even happens in my own writing. When I notice this is happening in my or my students' work, my recommendation is to create a "reverse outline." Instead of outlining what you *plan* to say, outline what you *did* say as if you are outlining someone else's article. This exercise can help you see where information can be merged and consolidated, which will improve your structure. It can also help you check you are using the hourglass format (see Figure 5.1).

Box 5.6: We know all the tricks

Both when writing your dissertation and later at work, almost 100 per cent of the people you send a document file to will having been using Word longer than you have. They will see right through changed margins, unconventional spacing and fonts. You aren't fooling anyone (well, maybe yourself). But that's OK. Most people don't really want to read a lot of text: it's OK to be concise.

Don't make your reader work hard

Have you ever read a paper where you had to back up and reread a sentence or paragraph again because you realized at the end something wasn't clear? Don't you hate that? I know I do! Just like when I choose to watch a feel-good summer blockbuster, I don't want to have to work hard to understand the material before me when I am reading. There are many ways you can minimize the workload for your reader – and I encourage you to do all of these.

Use parallel sentences

If you've explained one thing well and have to explain something similar or the complete opposite, using parallel sentences will help the reader detect the differences. Compare:

> On the first training block, participants saw each of the 24 pictures once in isolation with its name printed below it. Then, four pictures (b-, p-, l- and sh-initial items) were presented with the printed name in the center of the screen for the second block.

> "On the first training block, participants saw each of the 24 pictures once in isolation with its name printed below it. On the second block, they saw four pictures (b-, p-, l- and sh-initial items) and the printed name in the center of the screen."
>
> (McMurray, Aslin, Tanenhaus, Spivey & Subik, 2008, p. 1613).

This is a complicated experimental paradigm, but the second version (the published version) is clearer because the sentences follow a parallel structure: "On the __ block, participants/they saw ____ pictures" followed by the location of the printed name of the target picture. (Note that the first sentences in both examples are the same; for illustration purposes I did not cite these sentences in the top example, but see Box 5.1).

Keep the reader on the same page

You should know your study really well. You may know it well enough to take things for granted. But keep in mind that your study will be new to at least one person reading it. Thus, you may want to rephrase what you mean from time to time to ensure the reader is on the same page. One of my mentors is exceptionally good at this (in my opinion), and as I've read some of her papers I've found myself think-ing along and contemplating things like, "Oh, so this must mean . . ." only to find that her next sentence is almost something like, "So, this means . . ." As a reader it is wonderful to get this confirmation that you understand what the author is trying to communicate. Here are two examples:

> Items presented side by side can be compared by simply look-ing back and forth between them. Thus infants who look back and forth between the stimuli more have more opportunities to compare them.
>
> (Kovack-Lesh et al., 2008, p. 287).

What I like about this example is that the first sentence is abstract and general, but the elaboration in the second sentence provides a more concrete example of what the implications are for the target population and current method.

> All infants, regardless of condition, received a randomly selected set of six different items from the familiarization category. Thus, the design equated the number of items presented on each trial, the number of different items presented during familiarization, and the amount of exposure to each familiarization item.
>
> (Kovack-Lesh & Oakes, 2007, p. 75).

In this example the first sentence is very precise (six different items), which is especially useful if you want to replicate the authors. The sec-ond sentence explains the implications of what that information means in terms of understanding the design.

Minimize mental arithmetic

Obviously, your reader can do some mental arithmetic, but why make the reader work hard when you can do it? Which of the following would you rather read?

> Thirty-six undergraduate students participated for course credit. Data were excluded for five participants due to equipment error ($n = 2$) and failure to return for the post-test ($n = 3$).

> The final sample included data from 31 undergraduate stu-dents who participated for course credit. Data from five addi-tional participants were excluded due to equipment error ($n = 2$) and failure to return for the post-test ($n = 3$).

Avoid unconventional abbreviations

There are some abbreviations that are now part of most people's vocabulary (e.g. DNA, DVD, fMRI). However, unless you are abbreviating something anyone would recognize without reading your paper, avoid abbreviating.

If you must abbreviate something because it will be far too cumbersome for the reader if it is spelled out each time, be sure to introduce its full name with the abbreviation the first time you use it (e.g. Novel Noun Generalization Task [NNG]). If it has been a few pages you may want to include the long name again later just as a helpful reminder.

Box 5.7: It's all ~~Greek~~ Latin to me

If you are using a Latin abbreviation or phrase, check you understand the correct meaning:

i.e., In other words. Used to elaborate on a point, but not for examples: "In one group, children were read three different stories on each of 3 days (i.e., nine story exposures to nine different stories)" (Horst, 2013, p. 3).

e.g., For example. "Non-targets were familiar everyday items with monosyllabic names (e.g., car, bike, tree and sock)." (Breckenridge et al., 2013, p. 276).

cf., Compare, often used with negative connotation. Often used instead of "but see" to reflect differences in opinions or findings.

sic, Thus it was written, often used when there is a grammatical or factual flaw in the original quoted material, typically written [*sic*]. "it was not possible to select toys for 'either boys or girls' or for 'both boys and girls'. Instead, one could only select 'Boys [sic] Toys' or 'Girls [sic] Toys'" (Auster & Mansbach, 2012, p. 379). Here the flaw is the missing apostrophes (e.g. Boys' Toys).

verbatim, Word for word, "laptop note takers' tendency to transcribe lectures verbatim rather than processing information and reframing it in their own words is detrimental to learning" (Mueller & Oppenheimer, 2014, p. 1159).

a priori, Before the fact, usually used with "knowledge" or "experience": it is important that participants do not have a priori knowledge of the test items. Note, *a posteriori* is after the fact.

post-hoc, After, usually used with analyses that are completed after the main analyses.

Avoid generic names

Make the names of your conditions relate to your methods. Instead of condition 1 and condition 2 use something more informative like sleep-deprived group and control group or negative mood condition and neutral mood condition (see also Field & Hole, 2003).

Use the same terms throughout

This relates to repeating yourself. If there are multiple acceptable terms, pick one and use it consistently. Examples:

- Warm-up trials vs. training trials
- Toddlers or children
- 36-month-olds or 3-year-olds

Keep modifiers next to what they modify

Keep words that relate to each other near each other. Compare:

> This method only trains participants on one trial type.

> This method trains participants on only one trial type.

The second example is better because "only" relates to one single trial type (see also Griffies, Perrie, & Hull, 2013; Neuroscience, 2000).

Use short sentences

Griffies, Perrie and Hull (2013) suggest sentences be about twelve to seventeen words in length, on average.

Keep in mind what your reader doesn't know

As you write, also read through your paper from time to time to check that you are not discussing things you haven't yet mentioned to the reader (see also Field & Hole, 2003). Think carefully about what knowledge readers have as they get to each paragraph. For example, one of my students once wrote at the end of her introduction: "If repetition influences the learning of novel words, then children in the repeat group should perform better than children in the unique group." But as a reader I had not yet seen the method section to know what the conditions were called. The paper worked better after this sentence was changed to be more general: "If repetition influences the learning of novel words, then children who hear the same stories repeatedly should learn better than children who hear several different stories."

"One of the key skills I learned during my final year project was how to produce clear, accessible scientific writing. A small but highly valuable component of this was learning to not be afraid to repeat myself, and to regularly clarify points using concrete examples. As a first- and second-year student, I acted under the impression that it is of primary importance to include as much detail as possible into the set word limit, in an attempt to display a sheer volume of knowledge. In my first two years, I therefore sought to search for and cut out any sections of my essays and coursework which seemed repetitive in any way. As a reader, I now very much appreciate scientific writing which employs such techniques, and can actively critique writing which is unclear, inaccessible and therefore unconvincing, due to a complete lack of repetition and clarification. Furthermore, I learned the importance of highlighting the "big picture" at the start and the end of a scientific piece. I think this skill is undoubtedly one of the most important to learn, in order to produce work which is captivating and clear."

—Lauren H., BSc
PhD Student

Be concise

Concise writing involves using few words that are packed with meaning. It's a bit like fruit: tasty and sugary but packed with nutrition so that you really get something out of each relatively low-calorie bite. Writing concisely can also help you manage any page or word limits you might face.

If I simply told you "write concisely" that wouldn't be very practical advice. Where do you start? And do you even know if you are more on the concise or more on the verbose end of the spectrum? You can find ways to write more concisely by learning to avoid th-words, "helping verbs" and "empty phrases."

Avoid th-words

Although there are some very useful words that start with th- ("these data" and "theoretical" are both highly esteemed), "the," "this" and "that" are words you want to avoid.

The: When three-letter words are bad words

One easy way to make your writing more concise and professional is to avoid using "the." Seriously. Compare these two examples:

- The participants completed the test trials on a touchscreen computer.
- Participants completed test trials on a touchscreen computer.

Over the course of an entire paper "the" can really add up. An added bonus is that your reader will get to the important content words faster.

One way to avoid "the" is to use the plural form whenever possible. Compare:

- First, the participant completed the questionnaire on the computer. Then, the experimenter asked each participant if they [sic] noticed anything unusual about the questions. If the participant mentioned the font or font size, then the experimenter showed the participant a page of different fonts and asked the participant to recall the questionnaire font. (53 words)
- First, participants completed the questionnaire on the computer. Then, the experimenter asked if they noticed anything unusual about the questions. If participants mentioned the font or font size, then the experimenter presented a page of different fonts and asked them to recall the questionnaire font. (46 words)

Notice that the plural also helps avoid the problem that "he or she" is clunky but the participant is third person singular and "they" is third person plural so it is not grammatically correct to use "they."

This is so vague

On its own "this" is one of those words that makes readers work too hard. This what? This procedure? This finding? This theoretical perspective? Almost anytime you want to use "this" better, more informative – and more interesting – wording will be available (see also Griffies et al., 2013). Use the "find" function to identify where you have used "this" and replace it with what you really mean. Examples:

> *With This Alone:* "This comprises an attrition rate of 22%, which is similar to the rates reported for infant research (Slaughter & Suddendorf, 2007)."
> *With This Replaced:* "This attrition rate (27%) is similar to the rates reported for infant research (Slaughter & Suddendorf, 2007)."

With This Alone: "When children were presented with trials in which fewer coins equated to more money they performed significantly worse than chance. This is also true of trials in which the same number of coins equated to more money. Thus, children appear to attend to the number, not value, of coins."

With This Replaced: "When children were presented with trials in which fewer coins equated to more money they performed significantly worse than chance. They also performed worse than expected by chance on trials in which the same number of coins equated to more money. Thus, children appear to attend to the number, not value, of coins."

I have kept the final sentence from this excerpt to demonstrate a good example of both following statistics with a plain English sentence, p. 118 ("Thus, children . . ."), which is also a good example of keeping the reader on the same page, p. 128. To save even more words, the text could read: "In contrast, when presented with trials in which either fewer coins or the same number of coins equated to more money, children's accuracy was significantly worse than expected by chance, $t(11) = -4.39$, $p < .01$, $t(11) = -2.91$, $p < .05$, respectively."

With This Alone. The ANOVA confirmed significant improvements in performance between pre- and post-test, $F(2,28) = 6.91$, $p < .01$. This suggests that for both conditions test accuracy increased over time.

With This Elaborated: The ANOVA confirmed significant improvements in performance between pre- and post-test, $F(2,28) = 6.91$, $p < .01$. This improvement suggests that for both conditions test accuracy increased over time.

In this situation, I would even use "demonstrates" instead of "suggests."

That is a red flag

Although there are cases when you need to use the word "that" often it is a sign that you're concluding an "empty phrase" – see the next tip.

Avoid "empty phrases"

Unlike "empty calories," "empty phrases" are not tasty. In fact, they just make it take longer for your reader to read what you wrote, which can lead to inattention or even dislike.

Empty phrases are extra words added to a phrase or sentence that do not have any real content of their own (hence they are "empty"). For example, why write "A study by Smith and colleagues (2000) found . . ." when you can write "Smith and colleagues (2000) found . . ."? The latter is more to the point and will make your writing punchier and more exciting. It will help your writing to feel more "dense" (in the full-of-information sense) and less "fluffy." See Table 5.2 for examples.

Ask yourself if you can say it in fewer words

It's the twenty-first century, and everyone is busy. No one wants to spend longer than they have to reading *anything* from student dissertations to internal reports, to product descriptions, to "about us" pages on websites, or anything else that you might write after you graduate. Training yourself to use fewer words is a great transferable skill.

Several years ago I read Stephen King's memoir *On Writing* (King, 2000). A handful of images and ideas from that book have stuck with

TABLE 5.2

Examples of empty phrases, which are *underlined*. Notice they are really "empty": these sentences and phrases make just as much sense without them.

Wordy	Concise
It has been recognized that verbal input differs between high and low SES families (reference).	Verbal input differs between high and low SES families (reference).
It has been established that variability in the input aids children in learning to read (reference).	Variability in the input aids children in learning to read (reference).
It has been suggested that children are guided by a priori assumptions, including . . . [finding] (reference).	Children are guided by a priori assumptions, including . . . [finding] (reference). or Authors (year) argue children are guided by a priori assumptions, including . . .
It was predicted that if . . . then . . .	If . . . then . . .
According to [study], *it was found that* [finding]	According to [study], [finding].
. . .because *it has been found that* viewing different stimuli . . .	. . .because viewing different stimuli . . .
. . .were used *in order* to . . .	. . .were used to . . .
All objects *used throughout the trials* were approximately the same size.	All objects were approximately the same size.

me, among them the idea to aim to cut 10 per cent of your words in each subsequent draft. I don't literally count my own words to ensure I follow this rule, but the general idea that each draft should be shorter than the last is a good rule to follow.

As you are rereading your paper look for information that spans two sentences where you might be able to collapse the material into one sentence. Also look for information that is unnecessarily detailed for the purpose it is serving. For example, unless you are making a point about a flaw in another study, you will not need to tell your reader how many participants or trials were included in someone else's study that you are describing.

Choose phrases that lower your word count

There are several ways to lower your word count without sacrificing content (see Table 5.3).

- Watch out for variations of "be" and "have." These are helping verbs and often the verb they are helping can stand alone or there is something stronger that could replace them (see Table 5.3, examples 1–6).
- Watch out for word pairs that are redundant (see examples 7–10).
- The verb "to look" is also a red flag that you could use fewer words. It is also too casual for scientific writing (see examples 11–14).
- Other useful phrases to get you thinking about how you can reduce your words are provided in examples 15–30.

Use third person

You may have heard that you should not use the first person (I, we) in psychology writing. This is a rule that many professionals break but you should generally try to keep. Students often misunderstand this rule as "you should write in the passive voice," but third person and the passive voice are not the same thing. *Third person* puts the participants and the experiment first – and really, it is all about the participants and

TABLE 5.3		
Examples of wordy versus concise phrases		
	Wordy	*Concise*
1	Previous research has indicated that	Previous research indicates
2	It can be concluded that	Thus, *or* In conclusion,
3	In the current study, *it was tested to see* whether . . .	The current study *tested* whether . . .

	Wordy	*Concise*
4	Depending on which conditions participants were in they received different stimuli.	Participants received different stimuli depending on condition.
5	There is evidence to suggest that . . .	Evidence suggests . . .
6	*It would also be expected that* they should perform better on . . .	*Further,* they should perform better on . . .
7	Very important	Important
8	Both together	Together
9	Time delay	Delay
10	Delay period	Delay
11	Look at the possible effects	Investigate the possible effects
12	The current study aims to look at the effect of	The current study explores the possible effect of
13	This study looked at whether	This study tested whether
14	looked to address this	addressed this
15	Author, Author, Author and Author (2015) found	Author and colleagues (2015) found *especially useful for more than 3 authors.*
16	Due to the fact that	Because
17	Find out	Determine
18	Point out	Argue
19	Aimed to see	Assessed or Tested
20	Consisted of	Included
21	These authors focus on the argument	These authors argue
22	In the literature to date	In the existing literature
23	The study reported here will attempt to examine	This study will examine
24	*An additional aim of this study is to* establish . . .	*In addition, this study will* establish . . .
25	Participants were asked to read and sign the consent form.	Informed written consent was obtained.
26	for Condition 1 and Condition 2.	for both conditions.
27	It will *enable us to obtain* a baseline.	It will *establish* a baseline.
28	Prior to the experiment taking place	Prior to the experiment
29	Preschoolers were *used in this study* because . . .	Preschoolers were *tested* because . . .
30	Over the course of 10 trials	Across 10 trials

the experiment, isn't it? *Passive voice* takes away the action and makes it sound like things just happen without any control over the situation, but experiments are meant to be controlled. Compare these examples:

> *Passive Voice:* The questionnaire was completed by the participants before the main task.
>
> *Third Person:* Participants completed the questionnaire before the main task.
>
> *Passive Voice:* A touchscreen was used by the participants to answer the questions.
>
> *Third Person:* Participants answered the questions using a touch-screen computer.
>
> *Third Person:* Questions were presented on a touchscreen computer.

See how the third person gets the point across without being dry and without including "I" or "we"? As an added bonus, the third-person examples use fewer words.

Polishing: Little things to check at the end

- Double-check you use the same words to refer to your trial types (e.g. practice/training) and conditions (e.g. cookie-eating condition/ cookie condition) – and that these match your tables and figures.
- Double-check you have not duplicated your analyses (Harris, 2001). For example, if you have two conditions and Condition is a factor in an ANOVA, then do not also include an unpaired t-test (or paired t-test if condition is within subjects) because that would be providing redundant information.
- Ensure all of your test statistics are in italics (e.g., *t*, *F*, *r*, *p*, etc).
- Ensure any tables are numbered consecutively (only tables) and you actually refer to them in the text. Ensure the word Table is capitalized like a name.
- Ensure any figures are numbered consecutively (only figures) and you actually refer to them in the text. Ensure the word Figure is capitalized like a name.
- If you have numbered arguments, possibilities or explanations, make sure your "first, second, next, finally" words match the number of possibilities or explanations you said there were and that they are in order (in case you moved things around during editing).
- Use the "find" function to search for words you think you could use that your spell-checker won't notice (e.g. trail instead of trial; dependant instead of dependent).

- Use "find" to check you used "affect" as a verb and "effect" as a noun.
- Use "find" to check that your verbs are the plural form if you've written "data," which is plural (these data are, this datum is).
- Check all of your language is unbiased (i.e. gender neutral).
- Check ages are in digits (unless they're at the start of a sentence).
- Check novel names are in italics.

Helpful sentence structures and phrases

Here are some useful sentence structures:

Review = Authors + Method + Results + Optional Plain English Implication **Example:** Horst and colleagues (2011) read 3-year-old children the same or different stories over the course of one week. Children who heard the same stories learned more words than children who heard different stories. This supports the idea that contextual repetition facilitates word learning.

Review = Method & Results Condition 1 + Method & Results Condition 2 + Optional Plain English Implication + (Reference).
Example: Three-year-old children who are read the same stories over the course of one week learned more words than children who are read different stories, supporting the idea that contextual repetition facilitates word learning (Horst et al., 2011).

Summary = In the current study we explore [your topic]. Specifically, [subject group] [task] in one of [number] conditions.
Example: In the current study we explore contextual repetition. Specifically, 3-year-old children engaged in shared storybook reading in one of two conditions. → Then proceed to explain what participants did in the first condition and then the subsequent conditions.

Hypothesis = If [your topic] influences [thing you measure], then participants in [best condition] should [behavior you measure] better than [other condition].
Example: If contextual repetition influences word learning from storybooks, then children who hear the same stories should retain more words than children who hear different stories.

Second Hypothesis = In contrast, if [your topic] does not influence [thing you measure] then there should be no difference in [behavior you measure] between [conditions].

Example: In contrast, if contextual repetition does not influence word learning, then there should be no difference in word retention between children who hear the same or different stories.

Overall, these data demonstrate . . .
This research sheds light on . . .
This research provides novel insight into . . .
No other significant effects were found.

Box 5.8: Publishing your study

If your study works out and you obtain meaningful and significant results (congratulations!), you may consider publishing your paper. Faculty mentors are almost always first author on papers with student coauthors who are under the PhD level (see also Foreshaw, 2013). This is often appropriate because the supervisor may have come up with the original idea, spent a significant amount of time (re)analyzing the full dataset and (re)writing the manuscript so it is suitable for publication. Being a coauthor is still a great honor and demonstrates that you made a significant contribution to the paper. Consider the posters for *Good Will Hunting* (Van Salt, 1997). Just because Matt Damon's name was second after Robin Williams' name doesn't mean Matt Damon didn't give a superb performance. In some areas of psychology (especially on the biological end), the senior author is often the final author. This is more analogous to credits where the biggest star is listed last (e.g. "with Richard Attenborough" in the final credits of Jurassic Park, Spielberg, 1993). Both the APA and BPS have advice on determining authorship and your faculty mentor will know the conventions for your subfield.

In psychology it can take a very long time to get a paper published. A long time as in *years* – and this is after the data are all collected. First, a complete full draft of the manuscript must be written, then the authors determine which journal to send it to. Unlike publishing in some fields, manuscripts are only sent to one journal at a time, so the authors need to wait to hear back before sending the paper to another journal. Your faculty mentor can help you identify the best journal to approach first based on the topics it publishes and the members of its editorial board. Some authors also consider the journal's "impact factor," which is a citation matrix originally created as a quick way to estimate the influence of the papers each journal publishes. Just think of it as average citations per paper – but keep in mind that authors in different subfields publish (and therefore cite) papers at different rates, so a 4.0 impact factor might be very high for some subfields, but very low for others.

At the journal, the editor decides if the paper can be sent out for review. The editor should check to ensure there are no glaring flaws with the study or statistical analyses and also if the topic is a good "fit" for the journal's readership. At that point the paper is sent out for anonymous review, which means a handful of faculty at other labs provide written feedback on the paper. This process can take between one and four months, depending on the journal.

Once the reviews are returned, the editor decides whether or not to allow the authors to respond to the comments. If the editor rejects the paper the authors choose another journal and repeat the process (though often this is not overnight because all authors have moved on to another project). This can happen if the editor feels it is extremely unlikely the authors will satisfy the reviewers or if a flaw or lack of fit has been revealed. If the editor invites the authors to resubmit, they write a detailed reply to the reviewers indicating how they have addressed each concern (even the ones they thought were ridiculous) and the paper either goes back to the reviewers for more comments or the editor makes a final decision. Even if authors are invited to revise a paper, that does not guarantee it will be accepted for publication. The publication process involves a lot of rewriting and politics, which is why it is extremely, extremely rare to find students going it alone.

Once a paper is accepted for publication it is "in press," which means it is a fully creditable paper but has not yet been assigned a journal issue. At journals that still publish paper versions, the paper is literally being typeset and sent to a press. Once the paper has been assigned to an issue, you will cite it with that year, volume and issue. Until then, you can cite it as "in press."

Transferring these skills

Learning to write well for your dissertation is especially transferable because psychological writing is both clear and methodical. Clear, effective writing is a skill that you can use time and time again in a variety of jobs and even in your life outside of work (e.g. writing to your city council, complaining to a company about poor service). As your writing skills improve you will be able to craft stronger arguments and communicate your ideas clearly and succinctly, without extra wordiness that simply distracts from the point you are trying to make. Training yourself to stop using empty phrases and redundant words will serve you well when you need to write things for work with short notice. Avoiding the passive voice will help you to write catchy materials that grab your readers' attention and keep them engaged. Thus, the writing skills you are honing can help you to communicate effectively with potential and existing clients as well as coworkers and colleagues.

References

Auster, C. J., & Mansbach, C. S. (2012). The gender marketing of toys: An analysis of color and type of toy on the Disney store website. *Sex Roles, 67*(7–8), 375–88. doi: 10.1007/s11199–012–0177–8.

Bem, D., J. (1987). Writing the Empirical Journal Article. In M. P. Zanna & J. M. Darley (Eds.), *The Compleat Academic: A Practical Guide for the Beginning Social Scientist*. New York: Random House.

Bowers, J. S., Davis, C. J., & Hanley, D. A. (2005). Interfering neighbours: The impact of novel word learning on the identification of visually similar words. *Cognition, 97*(3), B45-B54. doi: /10.1016/j.cognition.2005.02.002.

Breckenridge, K., Braddick, O., & Atkinson, J. (2013). The organization of attention in typical development: A new preschool attention test battery. *British Journal of Developmental Psychology, 31*(3), 271–288. doi: 10.1111/bjdp.12004.

Cameron-Faulkner, T., Lieven, E., & Theakston, A. (2007). What part of no do children not understand? A usage-based account of multiword negation. *Journal of Child Language, 34*(2), 251–82. doi: 10.1017/S0305000906007884.

Columbus, C. (Writer). (1990). *Home Alone*: Twentieth Century Fox Film Corporation.

Field, A., & Hole, G. (2003). *How to Design and Report Experiments*. London: SAGE Publications.

Foreshaw, M. (2013). *Your Undergraduate Psychology Project*. Chichester, UK: British Psychological Society and John Wiley & Sons Ltd.

Gómez, R. L., Bootzin, R. R., & Nadel, L. (2006). Naps Promote Abstraction in Language-Learning Infants. *Psychological Science, 17*(8), 670–74. doi: 10.1111/j.1467–9280.2006.01764.x

Griffies, S. M., Perrie, W. A., & Hull, G. (2013). Elements of Style for Writing Scientific Journal Articles, *Publishing Connect* (pp. 1–7): Elsevier.

Harnad, S. (1990). The symbol grounding problem. *Physica D. Nonliear Phenomena, 42*, 335–346. doi: 10.1016/0167–2789(90)90087–6.

Harris, P. (2001). *Designing and Reporting Experiments in Psychology, Second Edition*. Maidenhead, UK: Open University Press.

Horst, J. S. (2013). Context and Repetition in Word Learning. *Frontiers in Psychology, 4*(149), 1–11. doi: 10.3389/fpsyg.2013.00149.

Horst, J. S. (2015). Word Learning via Shared Storybook Reading. In B. Küm-merling-Meibauer, J. Meibauer, K. Nachtigäller & K. J. Rohlfing (Eds.), *Learning from Picturebooks: Perspectives from child development and literacy studies*. London: Routledge.

Human, L. J., Biesanz, J. C., Finseth, S. M., Pierce, B., & Le, M. (2014). To thine own self be true: Psychological adjustment promotes judgeability via per-sonality–behavior congruence. *Journal of Personality and Social Psychology, 106*(2), 286–303. doi: 10.1037/a0034860.

King, S. (2000). *On Writing: A Memoir of the Craft*. New York: Simon & Schuster.

Kovack-Lesh, K. A., Horst, J. S., & Oakes, L. M. (2008). The cat is out of the bag: The joint influence of previous experience and looking behavior on infant categorization. *Infancy, 13*(4), 285–307. doi: 10.1080/15250000802189428.

Kovack-Lesh, K. A., & Oakes, L. M. (2007). Hold your horses: How exposure to different items influences infant categorization. *Journal of Experimental Child Psychology, 98*, 69–93.

Krameddine, Y. I., DeMarco, D., Hassel, R., & Silverstone, P. H. (2013). A novel training program for police officers that improves interactions with mentally ill individuals and is cost-effective. *Frontiers in Psychology, 4*(9), 1–10. doi: 10.3389/fpsyt.2013.00009.

Masarik, A. S., Conger, R. D., Donnellan, M. B., Stallings, M. C., Martin, M. J., Schofield, T. J., . . . Widaman, K. F. (2014). For better and for worse: Genes and parenting interact to predict future behavior in romantic relation-ships. *Journal of Family Psychology, 28*(3), 357–67. doi: 10.1037/a0036818.

McMurray, B., Aslin, R. N., Tanenhaus, M. K., Spivey, M. J., & Subik, D. (2008). Gradient sensitivity to within-category variation in words and syllables. Journal of Experimental Psychology: Human Perception and Performance, 34(6), 1609–31. doi: 10.1037/a0011747.

Miller, G. A. (1956). The magical number seven, plus or minus two: some limits on our capacity for processing information. *Psychological Review, 63*(2), 81–97. doi: 10.1037/h0043158.

Mueller, P. A., & Oppenheimer, D. M. (2014). The pen is mightier than the keyboard: Advantages of longhand over laptop note taking. *Psychological Science, 25*(6), 1159–68. doi: 10.1177/0956797614524581.

Neuroscience, N. (2000). How Experts Communicate. *Nature Neuroscience, 3*(2), 97. doi: 10.1038/72151.

Oakes, L. M., Coppage, D. J., & Dingel, A. (1997). By land or by sea: The role of perceptual similarity in infants' categorization of animals. *Developmen-tal Psychology, 33*(3), 396–407.

Pezzulo, G., Barsalou, L. W., Cangelosi, A., Fischer, M. H., McRae, K., & Spivey, M. J. (2011). The mechanics of embodiment: a dialog on embodi-ment and computational modeling. *Frontiers in Psychology, 2*(5), 1–21. doi: 10.3389/fpsyg.2011.00005.

Plumert, J. M., Kearney, J. K., & Cremer, J. F. (2007). Children's Road Cross-ing: A Window Into Perceptual–Motor Development. *Current Directions in Psychological Science, 16*(5), 255–58. doi: 10.1111/j.1467–8721.2007.00515.x.

Rayner, K., White, S. J., Johnson, R. L., & Liversedge, S. P. (2006). Raeding Wrods With Jubmled Lettres: There Is a Cost. *Psychological Science, 17*(3), 192–93. doi: 10.1111/j.1467–9280.2006.01684.x.

Scott, J., & Plagnol, A. C. (2012). Work-family conflict and well-being in Northern Europe. In J. Scott, S. Dex & A. C. Plagnol (Eds.), *In Gendered lives: Gender inequalities in production and reproduction.* Northampton, MA: Edward-Elgar Publishing.

Slaughter, V., & Suddendorf, T. (2007). Participant loss due to "fussiness" in infant visual paradigms: A review of the last 20 years. *Infant Behavior & Development, 30*(3), 505–14. doi: 10.1016/j.infbeh.2006.12.006

Spielberg, S. (Writer). (1993). *Jurassic Park*: Universal Pictures.

Van Salt, G. (Writer). (1997). *Good Will Hunting*: Miramax Films.

World Health Organization (2012). *Depression.* Geneva: World Health Organization (Fact sheet no.369).

6 Presenting your findings

I appreciate reading papers with (nice) tables and figures. Not just because it means that there are actually fewer words and not just because I'll be spared some rather boring sentences listing out statistics. Like anything written in APA style there are rules for tables and figures so I know I can get the information quickly – and often I remember articles better if I can recall what the tables and figures looked like. Perhaps this is why infographics are becoming so popular. Depending on what you do next, learning to create nice tables and figures could be one of the most useful transferable skills you gain from your research project.

Figuring out figures

Creating good figures is a skill. Like any skill, people differ in how much they enjoy doing it, how much of a knack they have for it and how much experience they have spent learning how to do it. This is why there are some really, really ugly figures out there and some figures that make people say things like, "Those data are beautiful!"

Keep in mind that, like your text, you want to mimic a professional journal article (p. 111). As you read papers if you see a paper with a really clear figure make a note to yourself in your lab notebook so you can go back and mimic that style when you create your own figure. Also note the average number of figures in your area.

Non-data figures

Figures are not just for presenting data. You may want to include a figure to depict the timeline of your experiment. For example, if you have a complex design you may want to include a figure to help the reader imagine what happened when. Figure 6.1 is an example of a computer-based procedure and Figure 6.2 is an example of a complicated timeline. Figures such as these can also be helpful for helping you to decrease your word count, but your main motivation for including such figures should be to help the reader understand your method. (To make Figure 6.2 I first created a table and used those cell lines as my guide to get

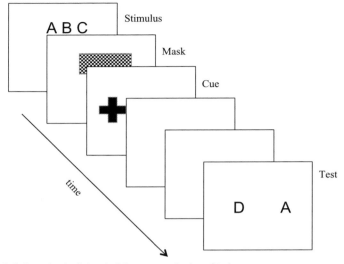

Figure 6.1 Example of a figure depicting a computer-based task

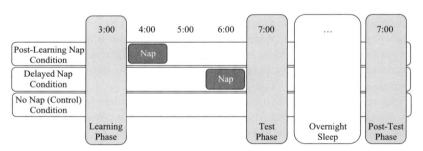

Figure 6.2 Example of a figure depicting a complicated procedure and design

the spacing of the time down. Later, when I didn't need the guidelines anymore I deleted the table.)

As you read papers related to your project you will begin to notice the conventions for depicting procedures similar to your own. For example, the convention for procedure figures for computer-based tasks is to use slightly overlapping rectangles representing what is shown on the screen at a given time (see Figure 6.1).

In addition to depicting your procedure, you may choose to show a schematic of the test space or apparatus. This could be helpful to the reader if locations are important to your study design, for example if you are showing where the participants sat relative to a confederate, depicting where the obstacles were placed in a landmark recognition study or if you have used a rat maze. It is also fairly common in developmental studies that use looking-while-listening procedures to depict where the speakers were relative to the screens and stimuli. In such cases, you should decide if it is more useful to take a photograph or more useful to create a drawing or schematic (these are typically drawn as if viewing the space from above, like when playing the board game Clue/Cluedo).

However, figures of your apparatus will not be necessary if you can explain all you need to explain in the text. Do not spend your time creating a test space or apparatus figure unless you really think it will add to the paper. If it doesn't help the reader understand something that could otherwise be unclear it is just a poor use of your time.

Finally, you may want to include a figure depicting your stimuli. This can be especially useful if you want to demonstrate that the stimuli were different during a learning phase but the same at test or the same during learning but different at test (see Figure 6.3 as an example).

If these are images displayed on a computer this is fairly straightforward because you just need to copy the same images. If these are physical objects the participants have interacted with you may want to take a photograph (see Box 6.1). Keep in mind that if you have many items you may not need to include every single one in your figure. Instead, your figure could include "a selection of the stimuli used in the current experiment."

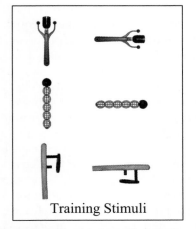 

Training Stimuli   Test Stimuli

Figure 6.3 Example of a figure depicting object stimuli

If you have multiple categories of stimuli, try to present them in a single figure with multiple panels (rather than including more smaller figures). The way I do this is to insert the individual images (usually one per panel) into PowerPoint. Then I create lines or unfilled boxes around the panels, add letters to title each panel and save the slide as a jpg (where to click to do that varies depending on the version of PowerPoint, but you can easily look that up for your version using Google). The advantage to this method is that the individual panels then move together as one item, which ensures the figure will not span a page break. (I also often use a really large font size [e.g. 18–22] so that when I paste the new figure into my document the font looks normal/not too small.)

Note, if your stimuli are text based (e.g. a list of non-words, a passage that is read, color words presented in a Stroop Task, etc.) you may just want to include a table or list. If the table is short enough this could go into the main document, but if it is very long you may want an appendix. But again, do not spend time creating such a table or list unless it will really add to the paper.

Box 6.1: A photograph is worth a thousand words

You may be using actual 3D objects in your study (maybe your participants are holding weights to see how that impacts handwriting, maybe your participants hold cooking tools in the Rubber Hand Illusion or maybe your child participants name objects). It can be especially helpful for the reader if you include a photograph of your objects as a figure in your method section.

There are two main styles of figures of objects. You can either create a figure with individual panels of each item that is equally sized (imagine a shopping website where you see a grid of pictures of similar products although they may be different sizes) or create a figure with all of the stimuli in one picture (imagine a magazine ad of a bundle of barbeque tools with the caption, "All this for only $9.99!"). There may not be a clear "right answer" to which kind of figure to choose. Generally, I use a grid style if all of the objects are approximately the same size and I have few enough that I can create a grid figure that will still fit on one page with the individual images a reasonable size. I use a collection when there are lots of objects or their sizes vary or I will be already including multiple panels (e.g. different stimuli for training and test trials in different panels of the same figure).

If you are creating a grid-style figure, photograph each object individually on a white background. Depending on the size of your objects this could be a stack of a few pieces of paper (the color of the table sometimes shows through a single sheet) or a large piece of poster paper. You may be able to use a portable photo stage like some sellers use on eBay. Learn from my mistakes: it may be tempting to lay the objects next to each other and move from one to the other instead of setting each object up, taking the photo, getting the next object ready, etc. I've experienced that the neighboring objects can sometimes interact with the camera's flash and make the background color less white and slightly tinted (e.g. you might get a very pale pink background if a neighboring object is red). It may also be tempting to create one large image, make duplicates and use a cropping function to create each individual image. But for submitting to journals I've discovered that the resolution of such figures is too low and I have to go back and retake the photographs.

If you are creating a collection-style figure, decide if you want to photograph the objects from above or from the side. If from above, you may want to stand on something to get a good angle. If from the side, you may want to use a backdrop like a large sheet of white card stock that can roll from the table to the wall so you don't have a horizontal line where the two meet. In both cases you may want to use tiny amounts of tape under the objects to keep them in an exact position.

A word of caution: if you also have a procedural figure, that figure likely includes some of your stimuli, so it may be redundant to include both a figure with the stimuli and a figure with the procedure. Readers do not like redundancy in figures, so you will probably want to just keep the procedural figure. If you really want both consider making one of them a table.

Raising the bar: creating data figures

What makes a good data figure? It all comes down to helping the reader get the important information quickly and accurately. For some students this means learning the art of "less is more." Even though you can make a figure with major grid lines and 3D bars does not mean that you should – unless it will improve accuracy for the reader.

If you are including multiple figures do your reader a favor and choose one color scheme or legend scheme (e.g. solid versus dashed lines) and use it the same way for every figure. What I mean is don't have one figure where the experimental group is navy and the control is cream and then later a figure where the experimental group is black and the control group is black-and-white striped or before is navy and after is cream, but there are different bars for the two conditions.

No matter how many figures you are including, set the font to the same style as your main text. If you do not change your font style it can look like you ran out of time writing your paper or you don't care (and if you don't care about that, did you care to do the consent procedure correctly? Or data entry?). It is good practice to have all of your figures the same size. Also use a large enough font size that the labels and y-axis values are still legible if you paste your figure into Word and need to shrink it to fit to within a page. You will also want to change the graph color scheme and not use the default colors from the program in which you made the figures. This can also raise flags about (lack of) attention to detail.

In some research areas it is common to include error bars that represent 1 standard error of the mean, while in others the custom is that error bars represent 95 per cent confidence intervals. Discuss with your mentor what your error bars (if you have them) should depict. Depending on your research area it may also be common to include a dashed line to indicate where chance or baseline performance is expected to be/against which readers should mentally compare your means (of course, you'll include statistics to make that comparison in the main text).

"I felt that doing the images figures was something not too demanding, so I chose to do them in the evening as I didn't have to 'think' as much but it made me feel like I'd made progress."

—Anna, BSc
English as a Second Language Teacher

The y-axis

The first thing to know about making data figures is what goes where: your y-axis should depict the values for your dependent variable (the thing you are measuring). It is often ideal to set the y-axis so that it spans from the minimum to maximum possible. For example, a lot of my research is analyzed in terms of proportion correct (possible range 0 to 1) so my y-axes are often from – you guessed it – 0 to 1.00. Even though the actual range of real scores might only be .40 to .70, by providing a y-axis that spans the entire possible range a reader is able to see how close my data are to ceiling (or floor), which would not be as easy to see if my y-axis started at .35 and ended at .80. It may initially feel like your data look more impressive if your y-axis only goes to .80 instead of 1.00, but many readers see through that and some may (even incorrectly) feel like the author is trying to trick them into thinking the data are better than they really are (think of all the times you see a product for only £4.98 instead of £5.00). Note, if your y-axis values include non-whole numbers (e.g. .5), change the number of decimal places to be the same for each value (e.g. .50, 1.00). You can often do this in a new menu that appears if you double-click on the y-axis.

Sometimes the dependent variable has no clear maximum (e.g. number of Facebook friends, amount of money gambled away, number of cigarettes smoked). In this case, just set y-axis maximum to a value close to your highest mean + its standard error (if you are including error bars) and round up to a number that will work well with your tick-marks. For example, if your highest mean + 1 standard error = 21, you may want to set the y-axis to go up to 25 but if for some reason you want to have tick marks at 4, 8, 12, 16 . . . you might choose 24.

Some dependent variables can be negative, so you may need your y-axis to span from a negative number to a positive one. Here, it is not always necessary for the minimum to be as far from 0 as the maximum (e.g. you might want .-25 to +75 but not necessarily –75 to +75).

When you label your y-axis do not label it "mean" or "average" something. It is not showing the mean: the marker on the line or the top of your bar is showing the mean. The y-axis is showing a range. Just label it whatever you measured in your study (e.g. proportion of words learned, number of cigarettes smoked).

Always include a unit of measurement (trials, cm, etc.) on your y-axis.

Excel and other software programs will often default to providing a lot of values for your tick marks, e.g., 5, 10, 15, 20 . . . 95, 100. This will make a figure look cluttered and even worse, it makes it harder for the reader to draw a mental line across to get a sense of what the means are. Set a reasonable value for the distance between tick marks. Often authors will choose a value to divide the y-axis into quarters or fifths. If your y-axis is a count of something less than 15 (e.g., range 0–12) you may want to have a mark at every even number.

Figure 6.4 depicts hypothetical data for a pretend study in which coffee- and non-coffee-drinking students took lecture notes either by

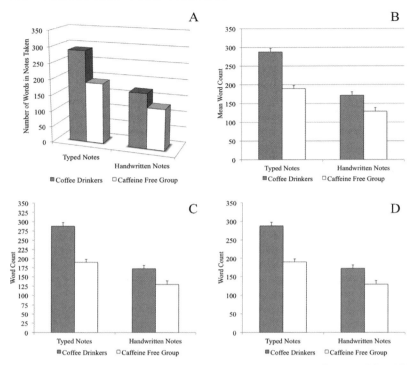

Figure 6.4 Examples of very poor (Panel A), poor (Panel B), slightly poor (Panel C) and good (Panel D) attempts at presenting the same data in a bar graph

hand or using a laptop. Panel A is the kind of figure you really want to avoid. It is fun to look at, but the 3D format does not allow for error bars, the y-axis title is too long and the bars and stripes make the figure too busy. Panel B is a little improvement but refers to the y-axis as the mean, although the means are the height of the bars. Panel C has a good y-axis label and looks more professional in that there are no major gridlines, but there are too many values on the y-axis making the figure again too busy. Finally, Panel D depicts a figure for these kinds of data in a style you would commonly see in a journal article.

Finally, if you have multiple figures with the same dependent variable keep the y-axis the same size across all of the figures so the reader can easily compare. For example, if your y-axis needs to go up to 25 for Experiment 1 but really only 20 for Experiment 2 (maybe those participants never did as well), make both go up to 25 so that the reader can more easily compare between the figures.

"Learning how to create a clear, visually appealing and informative graph is a skill I have carried with me throughout the past three years and has helped greatly in giving presentations. I believe that learning this skill early on was of huge benefit to my presentation skills at master's level and beyond."

—Lauren H., BSc
PhD Student

Lines or bars or other?

Before we discuss the x-axis it's important to make sure you are creating the right *kind* of figure (e.g. line graph, bar graph).

Line graphs are pretty and they are arguably easier to understand because you just need to see if the lines are parallel for a main effect or intersect (or would intersect if you kept drawing them) for an interaction. Unfortunately, not all data should technically be depicted with a line graph. Knowing when line graphs are OK is especially tricky nowadays because a noticeable minority of published papers include line graphs when they shouldn't. Line graphs are kind of like speed limits: no one has problems when they make perfect sense (e.g. heavy rain), a lot of people think the rule applies to others and not to them – and just because "everyone" disobeys the rule doesn't make it right.

Here is a handy rule of thumb. Recall from geometry that a line is just a series of dots (i.e. data points). If all of the data points making a given line are from the same participants then it's probably OK to use a line graph. If some of the data points making a given line are from one group of participants and some from another or even multiple other groups: don't use a line graph.

Here are some examples with common factors:

- Age: if age is a within-subjects factor then it's OK to use lines (for example if you are conducting part of a larger study and following children through multiple grades or ages). In contrast, if age is between-subjects, for example you are dividing your participants into different groups (e.g. tweens vs. teens, 18 vs. 21), then you must use bars.
- Time: if time is a within-subjects factor then it's OK to use lines (e.g. trial number or you tested everyone repeatedly at set points). However, if you varied time between-subjects (e.g. one group was

tested immediately, another after a short delay and another after a long delay), then you must use bars.

- Conditions vary in number: You may have a between-subjects design where the groups are different along a measureable continuum. For example, two students and I once ran a study where we varied how many distractor objects (2, 3, 4) were present when children heard new words (Horst, Scott, & Pollard, 2010). But it's still between-subjects and still calls for bars. (Just think of my example; I couldn't really have 2.75 objects so it's not continuous.)
- Conditions vary in complexity: You may have a between-subjects design where you increase something between groups (e.g. number of cigarettes smoked per day or number of distractions while the participants completed a timed-IQ test). Still between-subjects, still bars (handy mnemonic (p. 85): between-subjects and bars both begin with B).

Keep in mind that there are more alternatives to a line graph than a traditional bar graph. If the range of responses is important for your study you may want to use a "bars and whiskers" graph. If the individual responses are important for your research question you may want to include dots to show where the outliers are or a scatterplot. Some scatterplots also convey additional information about condition or trial types by using different colors, shapes or letters to show which data points are from different samples or trial types.

Box 6.2: How much data per figure

Depending on the amount of data you are presenting, you may need to consider if you need multiple figures to make the data easier to see and therefore understand.

Generally, if you have more than 6 or 8 bars in a bar-graph the individual bars will be too narrow to differentiate (especially for readers with poor eyesight). If you have a 2×2×2 design (8 bars) you may want two panels of 4 bars each.

If you have factors within factors (e.g. pre- and post-test and then conditions), it can be helpful to have the lines differentiating the segments of the x-axis go all the way down to be level with the bottom of the x-axis labels.

Keep in mind, however, that if your tasks are different and the scores are not on the same scales (different minimum and maximum possible) you will need separate figures. Though, you may want to consider converting the scores to proportions or percentages, which can put them back onto the same scale.

Histograms are not traditional bar graphs and readers are generally OK with more than 8 bars in such figures, often because they are looking at the shape of the "curve" not scanning for main effects and interactions.

The x-axis

In many cases what to put on your x-axis may be quite straightforward. If the y-axis depicts your dependent variable, then the x-axis must depict your independent variables or your factors. If you only have one factor (e.g. year at university, task difficulty, smokers vs. nonsmokers), then obviously this goes on your x-axis. If you have two factors (e.g. year at university and typing speed) then you need to decide which factor is more important for the argument you are making. You may want to try the figure with one factor along the x-axis and the other presented by different lines/bars and the other way to see which version makes your key result "pop." The APA (2010) dictates to put the things you are comparing next to each other.

Imagine a study with a 2×2 design such as participants learn keypresses for 75 3-note melodies and are trained with either background music or silence and then have disturbed or good sleep. Figure 6.5 shows two ways to present these hypothetical data. Panel A shows sleep condition on the x-axis and a legend for training condition. Panel B shows the reverse. The interaction is apparent in both versions of the figure (imagine a line from where the error bars touch the top of one white bar to where the error bars touch the top of the other white bar and a similar line on the gray bars: the lines would cross, forming a kind of X,

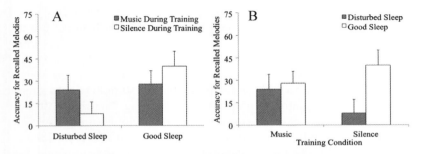

Figure 6.5 Two examples of presenting the same data that highlight different effects

just like an interaction in a line graph). The means and standard errors in both panels are identical, however, they highlight different aspects of the data. Panel A highlights that participants who had disturbed sleep are generally performing worse than participants who had good sleep. In contrast, Panel B highlights that the kind of sleep you get makes a huge difference if you trained in silence but only a little difference if you trained with music. The same data but different "stories." Decide what the story is that you want to tell to determine which way to present your data. (Note, for Panel B, I made an x-axis title "Training Condition" because "Music During Training/Silence During Training" looked too cluttered and was highly repetitive.)

Box 6.3: Using multiple figures and tables

Figures and tables can be useful for the reader and fun to create, but you do not want to include so many figures that the results section is difficult to follow or your results section continues for many pages (see also, APA, 2010). If that is a concern either include multiple panels, move the table/figure to an appendix or simply put the information in the main text.

If making multiple panels would make your figure too difficult to decipher or the information really isn't needed at the same time, then go ahead and use multiple figures (the same holds true for tables). Consider where you place your figures carefully. Real journal manuscripts often include all of the tables and figures at the end, but some journals – and department policies – recommend putting the figures and tables in the text where the reader will need them. If this is the case, try to have each table or figure at the top of the page on or after you tell the reader "see Figure X" (you may need to insert a textbox in Word and then drag and drop the figure or table into there).

Number your tables and figures consecutively from where you first mention them. Books and monographs often have multiple chapters so they use non-whole numbers (e.g., Table 6.1 or Figure 2.1) but for your project you will want to use only whole numbers unless you have a figure with multiple panels (e.g., "see Figure 2a" or "see Figure 2, Panel A"). Note, your tables and figures lists are independent of each other. For example, if you first refer to a stimulus figure, then a table with preliminary information, then a big data figure, these will be Figure 1, Table 1, Figure 2, respectively (not Figure 1, Table 2, Figure 3!). If you have an appendix, re-start your numbering with an A (e.g. Table A1) (if for some reason you have multiple appendices, restart again, e.g. Table B1).

Remember that each figure caption must stand alone. Even though it is a bit boring and repetitive, you must repeat all of the information needed to understand each figure in its caption. This is *not* the place to say "All aspects of the [analysis] were the same as in Experiment 1." It is very frustrating to readers if they have to flip to another part of the document to understand the section they are currently reading – and with copy-and-paste how hard is it, really?

Box 6.4: Down the line: Think before you print

There are some things that just have to be printed, e.g., court notices, wedding invitations – your dissertation . . . . Even if you email someone your dissertation (or a file you create at your next job), there is a chance someone else will print it out or photocopy it. You may create it with the intention that the reader will see it in black and red, but keep in mind the reader might only see a copy printed in grayscale on economic mode. How do you cope with that? Still use color. Color will make the figure "pop." But, add in some redundancy in case of grayscale.

Bar graphs can look quite elegant in black and white (e.g. some black bars and some white bars) or dark gray and white. But you may want to use other colors (it might even be relevant, for example if you are conducting a study on different grocery store chains). If you choose other colors simply ensure that they are not the same *lightness*. For example, if you want green and yellow, include a deep green and light yellow as your fill colors.

Some line graphs will also work in just black and white, for example one solid line and one dashed line. However, you might have more than two lines or want a small enough figure that you are unsure if the reader will perceive that one line is in fact dashed. Do not use lightness (e.g. paler colors) as your redundant factor for line graphs! You will risk the line being printed so faintly that it will be too tiny for the reader to follow (always assume your reader has poor eyesight).

Instead, vary the *weight* of your lines. For example, I once created a line graph where the blue lines had a weight of 2 points and the red lines had a weight of 4 points (in most programs if you double click on the line a window will come up where you can find a "weight" drop-down menu). In the text we even referred to them as "thin blue" and "thick red" lines in case the reader had printed the paper in grayscale (Williams & Horst, 2014). If you must use dashed lines do check that when printed in economic or grayscale modes that there are still spaces between the lines (i.e. the line is still dashed).

Tables

Figures are handy, but depending on the information you have a table may be better (you should definitely not have both a table and a figure with the same information). Tables are typically used for demographic information (e.g. age, vocabulary scores, income levels), information conveyed in text form and for some specific analyses (e.g. regression). Tables can be especially helpful if you want to compare two groups on a variety of measures, in particular when those are on different scales. The APA (2010) provides many examples of different types of tables, including flowcharts and complicated regression models.

Tip: When is a table a figure?

Just because you have rows and columns does not mean you have created a table. If there is any form of illustration (e.g. images of brain scans, drawings of stimuli) you should refer to your "table" as a "figure" (APA, 2010).

The small print, i.e. captions

You need a caption for every figure and for every table. In an ideal world, your reader will wait to look at the figure or table until you direct him/her to do so (e.g., "see Figure 2" or "As can be seen in Figure 3"). Unfortunately, readers like tables and figures and may skip ahead to look at the figures or tables when they get to the Results section. This can be problematic if you do not have good captions because the reader might not know what he is looking at or she might misunderstand (this is also one of the many reasons why it's so useful to be consistent with your condition names, especially from methods section to results section). Another way to think about this is that you need to design your figures, tables and their captions so that someone can understand them *without* having read your results section.

The first "sentence" of your caption should work as a brief title. It should inform the reader what the content in the table or figure is.

Examples:

* Book genre preferences for each condition.
* Stroop task performance as a function of sleep deprivation.
* Non-word repetition accuracy from Experiment 1.

Keep the figure title short. It can be tempting to just write one long sentence (e.g. "Book genre preferences for the eBook reading condition, depicting in black, and the traditional book reading condition, depicted in red."), but this can make things harder later if your department has special formatting guidelines – plus, it's harder on the reader and less like what a professional journal article is like.

Although you should keep the title short, you should still include all of the details necessary to understand the figure (e.g. which condition is depicted in black and which in red). Simply include additional sentences. Because this is a caption, you may write more concisely than you would in the main text (e.g. "Data from the eBook and traditional book reading conditions are depicted in black and red, respectively.").

If you have additional symbols or aids (dotted line, error bars, asterisks) spell out for the reader what these mean. The conventional practice is to use one * for $p < .05$, two for $p < .01$, three for $p < .001$, etc. – but still explicitly state that you did this: it allows the reader to confirm that you know what you are doing. It is especially important to note what your error bars mean because some subfields conventionally use one standard error of the mean while others tend to use 95 per cent confidence intervals – this can have severely negative consequences for data interpretation if your reader assumes you used error bars for one of these but you really used them for the other!

Avoid abbreviations in your captions (APA, 2010). Remember the reader might look at the figures early and not know the abbreviations yet. Also, do not mention the actual results (e.g. do not include "There was no significant difference between groups" or "The figure indicates a main effect of test delay."). This information belongs in the main text. Your reader is likely a faculty member who has seen enough figures to tell by eye if you have a main effect or not and can then read the results section to confirm if she is correct.

Presentations

As part of completing your project, you may have to give a talk or oral presentation. By now you have likely seen a lot of lectures, student presentations and maybe even some external speakers' seminars. You may have an idea of some of the major problems that make for a bad talk: little or no eye contact, mumbling or speaking such that it's hard to understand, reading directly from slides, too much information on slides, spending too much time on individual slides, not defining jargon as it comes up, etc. Those are obviously things that you do not want to do, but what do you want to do to create a stellar presentation?

Slide and content format

As you design presentations keep in mind that PowerPoint can do a lot of things that you don't necessarily need it to do, so don't go overboard. I highly recommend that you use a white background for all of your presentations. It can be pleasant for people to read, if the projector you are using is acting temperamental, it is less likely to mess up white than another color and most images and figures you will want to insert will have a white background, so where and how you paste things in will be easier. For example, you might want to re-label an axis of a figure for which you do not have the original file. If you use a white background you can easily paste a white box over the original label and then type your own.

Box 6.5: The power of PowerPoint: clever things PowerPoint can do for you

- **Align text or images.** Use this to make sure items are at the same level (top, bottom, left, right, center, middle can each be aligned).
- **Guidelines.** Use a grid or guidelines that you can move to ensure items are really aligned. This is especially helpful if you have a textbox or item that has some white space and you do not want to align with the actual top but what looks like the top.
- **Group items.** Use this to make multiple images or several shapes that together form an image or other items a "group." Benefits include: facilitates animation (e.g. all of your legend info could come up at once) and facilitates moving because everything will move together as one unit.
- **Change the background color for a single slide.** This is useful for using videos (black background can help the material show up better) and if you want to color code to yourself that a slide still needs editing (p. 96).

Show your true colors

During your degree each of your presentations might be on a different topic and might be very different to each other, but after you graduate you may be giving presentations that build on each other or are very similar (e.g. how our client outreach has improved every month). You can save yourself a lot of effort by choosing a color scheme and general style and using the same style over and over again. It may sound boring to use the same style all the time, but it really saves time and energy because it's one or more fewer decisions to make before every presentation. Personally, I find that many of the preprogrammed slide formats/designs in PowerPoint start the main text or bullet points too low, so I made my own "style" (but you can hardly call it that because it is too basic). I just center the heading in red in font size 44 with the top of the heading box flush with the top of the slide. Then my bullet points are in font size 28 (32 whenever possible) in the same font but black. When I add references I add them in a smaller font size, because I figure there are two types of people in the audience: those who couldn't care less about my references and won't read them and those who are interested enough in my references that they will either already know them or be willing to look very closely for a moment to get the reference.

Sometimes in longer presentations if you will be presenting multiple data slides or multiple results summaries it can be helpful to color-code the conditions each time you mention them (you can even color code your figures to match). For example, imagine you have two groups (e.g. social drinkers and nondrinkers) and will present data from four different measures. It can be helpful for the audience to compare and keep track of the groups if you consistently keep the data for one group blue and data for the other group green and if you change the font color for the groups when you write them out (e.g., if you had the bullet point "social drinkers scored significantly higher on the extraversion measure than nondrinkers" you might have "social drinkers" in blue and "non-drinkers" in green). This works especially well if you want to make the point that one group always performed better than another group across every measure.

"Presenting our initial proposals to the group enabled us to develop our presentation skills: adapting our communication style from that which you would use informally with participants to a style more suited to addressing an academic audience. It was through presentations like these that I realized one of my key strengths was presenting, and this helped me to focus my job search, knowing this was an area that I enjoyed."

—Rosa, BSc
Senior Program Manager (Charity Sector)

Put up a brave font (not really)

Choose one font (possibly with two styles, e.g. bold and regular) and use it consistently. Do not use multiple fonts on the same slide unless they serve a real purpose (e.g. for qualitative data you may want to have quotes from different individual participants in different fonts). Sans serif fonts (e.g. Arial, Helvetica, Calibri) are easier to view at a distance and should be used for presentations, while serif fonts (e.g. Times New Roman, Garamond, Minion) are best for documents and blocks of text.

A good rule to aim for is to have your main text/bullet points in at least 28 point font size. At first when you start working with font size 28 it may feel enormous on your screen; after all you can probably read font size 12 just fine. Keep in mind, though, that the font size isn't for you; it's for the audience. Importantly, it is for everyone sitting in the back row. If the audience members in the back row cannot read your bullet points (even though they should be listening to you as well), they may become bored or confused and you don't want that. With font in size 28 you can usually fit about five or six bullet points on each slide. That's plenty. By the time you have covered about six points the audience will probably welcome a bit of visual change and enjoy that you move on to the next slide. Five to six bullet points will also allow you to have plenty of "white space," which is visually appealing and appreciated by audience members.

Warning: computers think they are clever and will often adjust your font size for you to fit everything you write onto one slide. This is *not* a case of making the computer work for you. Rather, this is something you want to watch out for and really keep an eye on as you make a presentation!

Tip: Captions in presentations

If you are giving an oral presentation you will still need to convey to the audience the information that would have been in your figure captions (e.g. "the dotted line represents chance performance" or "error bars depict 95 per cent confidence intervals"). Often this can be done verbally as you explain the figure.

Animation

There are two reasons why you should include some animation in your presentations: one is to keep your audience's attention where you want it and the other is to help yourself. When you animate, keep in mind that it's all about the content. You are trying to convey information not show how well you can choose different items from a drop-down menu in your software. Like your fonts and color schemes, you want to use as few different styles as possible, be consistent and only use what you have to in order to get your point across. Do not animate at the level of individual words or letters (that's obnoxious) and keep in mind that you can often change the timing so (a) things appear at the same time as each other, which is really helpful for sub-bullet points and (b) so things that grow or move can be faster/slower to suit your needs.

Tip: The end

At the end be sure to thank your mentor and everyone on your team and external funding (if applicable). You can just list these individuals on an acknowledgements slide. If someone is a coauthor of the presentation, he or she should not be listed in the acknowledgements (that's like saying, "I thank myself."). I often title my final slide "Thank You" and then have a smaller heading of acknowledgements on the same slide. I recommend not putting "Any questions" or something like that on the slide because someone might want to say a few words before the questions.

For the audience

Imagine you have a slide with five bullet points of content. You likely want to animate it so that each bullet point comes up one at a time. If you put everything up there at once, you risk that someone – maybe even most people – in the audience will keep reading even if you are only telling them about Bullet Point 1 or 2. That someone might be so concerned about understanding Bullet Point 5 that he isn't even listening to you and missing some critical information that will cloud his understanding of what comes later.

Even if everything is crystal clear, if someone reads ahead she could finish learning all of the content from the slide quite a while before you finish the slide, which can make her feel bored and like your talk was "slow" or "boring" even if that's not true.

For the presenter

Animation isn't just for your audience; it's also a tool for you as the presenter. Again, imagine you have a slide with five bullet points of content. You are going to be a lot less likely to accidentally skip a point or to accidentally tell the audience the material in the wrong order if you animate each point as you go. It's kind of like, when you click the computer is telling you want to do: "Now, tell them about how you recruited the participants!" "Now, mention the main effect is significant!" "Now remember to tell them about that super cool implication you don't want to forget!"

Personally, I use animation for more than just bullet points – but sparingly and still professionally. For example, after I gave my first few talks I realized that I was developing a bad habit of just jumping into my first results without telling my audience what they were about to see in the graph. If the presenter and audience are coming from different areas of psychology or different areas of expertise even within the same subarea, it can save a lot of confusion to just take a moment to point out, "The y-axis depicts . . . and the x-axis depicts . . . ." Now, I rarely forget to tell my audience what is y and what is x on my figures. It's not because I'm remembering; it's because I'm using animation cleverly.

I make a duplicate of my first data slide, remove the bullet points summarizing the findings, then remove the data from the graph and all of the extras like *s for p-values. I'm left with a brief moment with a blank graph that only has the y- and x-axes. When I see that I know my computer is telling me, "Tell them what the y-axis is! And the x too!"

In another talk I gave years ago I also wanted to ensure I didn't forget what was different between two simulations I was presenting. So, when I created the slide about the second simulation I actually added a yellow star-like shape that said *New!* like you might see in bad commercials. That gimmicky star was the only thing that came up on its assigned click, but it was a great reminder to me to tell the audience, "Importantly, what is different in this simulation is . . . ."

Sometimes when animating it can also be helpful to have things almost anywhere on the slide just to get the animation order correct (especially if things have to disappear as something appears). Once the animation order is correct, then you can move things to their final positions. I find this technique especially useful if I have multiple bits of text that I want to appear (and disappear) in sequence, but I want them all located in the same position on the slide (though see the end of Box 6.7 for an alternative lower-tech solution).

Box 6.6: Animate in reverse

Once in a while you might want to animate something really tricky or complicated. I've learned that it's often easier in such situations to "animate in reverse."

For example, one of my favorite figures is a line graph from a study where we tracked children's word retention over the course of one week (Williams & Horst, 2014). When I give talks that include that figure I don't like to have the whole graph exposed at once because I want to reveal the findings to the audience step by step (there were four time points). I figure it would take me days (at least) to figure out how to make the lines "grow" and end up where they are supposed to (if my software can do that at all). So, my cheat is to do the reverse: for that figure I made squares without shadows and filled them with white. Then I have them animated to disappear by wiping to the right when I click. The end result is that it looks like my lines are growing. This didn't take days, but it still took a while. I had to zoom in really high (e.g., 300 per cent) and make sure the boxes lined up so that I didn't have any part of the lines peeking through and so I wasn't hiding things too long (you want the right edge of a box to line up with the right edge of the marker it is going to reveal). To get the positions just right I changed the boxes to somewhat translucent until I was done and then changed them to completely solid at the end.

If you want to reveal bars on a bar graph one at a time you can also use white boxes that disappear or wipe away when you click. In fact, it can look rather impressive if you have such a box wipe from the bottom because it makes it look like the bar is growing. I've used this method when I've wanted to really highlight that one group surpassed another group, though I usually just have the boxes disappear on each click, so the whole bar seems to appear at once. If you are using such boxes with bar graphs, do be careful to zoom in and align things on the x-axis.

Finally, keep in mind that in most cases no one will count your slides. Sometimes the easiest and most effective way to "animate" something is to simply have multiple slides that look like one slide with new things appearing as you click. If you just want things to appear without any fancy wiping or dissolving you may want to use this approach.

Multi-media

Whenever possible take advantage of how a presentation is different from a document. Specifically, add photos of your stimuli and apparatus when you can and photographs of people or related concepts to illustrate your point (e.g. if your talk is about anxiety you can include a photograph of people wringing their hands and biting their lips; if your talk is about relationships you could show a couple walking along a beach). Ask your supervisor if he or she has images you can use or if looking for one online go to the settings in Google (there is a gear icon or settings button) and under "usage rights" choose "free to use or share, even commercially" to avoid copyright infringement.

Depending on your research topic, it may be useful to show a video of your task. This can be helpful if you are using a method that requires the participant to do something (e.g. point to a location blindfolded, delay gratification, recall a previous experience in an interview), but is likely unhelpful if you are using a questionnaire or a well-established standard method (e.g. Stroop task) that could be boring to watch.

Of course, you *may only* show the video footage of a participant completing your task if you have informed consent to do so (you may have included this on your consent form; if not, try to contact a participant whose footage you would like to use). If you do not have consent to show such footage, you could ask a friend or fellow lab member to consent to being videotaped completing the task so you have some footage to show in your talk.

When showing footage of a real participant remember to keep his or her identity confidential (e.g. explain "This man is about to give directions to the main campus library" or "This child was told not to eat any marshmallows until the experimenter returned," not "John is about to . . . " or "Margot was told . . . .").

One common mistake about using videos is showing clips that are too long. It is OK to crop your clips and only show key trials or moments. For example, the strange situation task lasts about twenty minutes, but really only about a minute (or less) would be necessary for the audience to get the general idea of what you coded.

 ### Tip: Sound

Whenever possible try to choose video clips where sound is helpful but not necessary. Computers can be very fickle so you should not take for granted that the sound will work when you give a presentation. Usually sound works fine, but be prepared to narrate any videos you plan to show.

Being nervous

When you give a talk it's natural to be nervous. One thing that has really helped me to feel less nervous is to remind myself: *this isn't Shakespeare.* Now, I'm not saying this to imply that the talk isn't stunning, exciting and all-out brilliant. What I mean is: the audience does not have the

script memorized. If you were reciting Hamlet's "to be, or not to be" mono-
logue (Shakespeare, 1600), someone in the audience could actually know
the words you are supposed to say better than you. But this isn't Shakespeare. No one knows what you are supposed to say and the order you are
supposed to say it in. OK, your faculty mentor might be a close second, but
that person wants to see you succeed. Meanwhile, if you mean to tell the
audience about who your participants were and then how you recruited
them, but you accidentally tell them about recruitment first, that's OK! Just
tell them who the participants were next.

Until you have given a talk many, many times or have given dozens
of talks it is also somewhat common to forget something or remember
after you've moved on. (Have you ever heard someone say, "Oh, I meant
to tell you earlier" or "I should have pointed out"?) It's probably better to say something late than never, but adding side comments like, "I
should have said this earlier" can sound unprofessional and point out a
flaw other people may not have even noticed. If this happens to me (and
it doesn't very often now, see Animation, above) I try to use "Also, note
that . . . " and then tell them what I should have said earlier. Again, it's
not Shakespeare – the audience won't know if your lines are out of order.

To appear less nervous, try to practice your talk. Ideally, practice more
than once with different people – it's far too easy if you practice with the
same person to just fudge it – "Oh, I forgot the part on the ANOVA. Well,
you heard it before . . . " Do keep in mind, however, that you don't need
to take all of the advice people will offer – but do always listen to your
faculty mentor or someone who knows how you will be evaluated!

Also try to avoid adding useless words such as "like" or "um" that
can highlight how nervous you are. One thing you can try is to just take
a breath or exhale instead of letting yourself say "um." Over time saying
"um" will be less of a habit.

"Receiving and responding to feedback (whether verbal or written)
was so useful in university. This made me reflect and evaluate my
own work from another person's perspective and also encouraged me
to think outside the box more. I use this at work when communicating with my manager, supervisor and colleagues so that I am able to
identify my own learning needs and improve my working practice."
—Tash, BSc
Senior Occupational Therapy Assistant.

Talking about your study

Depending on your department's policies you may need to answer questions after your presentation or even give an oral defense (viva voce) of some sort (in which case definitely discuss what to expect with your supervisor as procedures vary across departments). Before you panic about the questions you might be asked, please note:

- *No one knows your study better than you.* Your supervisor might know the literature or rationale for some stats better, but having done the testing you know the methods better than anyone (you were right there during testing).
- Most questions are asked for clarification. Some, if not most, of these will actually be easy questions if you know your study well. (How many trials did you have? What order did they do the tasks in? Why did they do that task first?)
- Many questions are asked because the questioner is genuinely interested in how the findings apply to his or her own research or what he or she knows about psychology. Most people asking questions want to know more.
- It's OK to ask someone to repeat a question. Often when people repeat questions they elaborate or rephrase the question, which might give you a better idea of what they are asking (as well as more time to think of an answer!).
- It's OK to not have an answer. Sometimes people ask a I'm-just-curious question and there isn't a definite answer so you can just speculate: "I don't know how tri-lingual blind individuals would behave in this task, but given what I know about bilingual language . . . ." Sometimes people forget details: "I don't recall how many participants asked for the instructions to be repeated, but I can look it up." Sometimes people haven't read a paper: "I'm not familiar with King's work on that, but I'll look it up. Thank you for the reference." Just be honest. It's much better to admit you don't know something than to fake an answer and get caught.
- Eye-contact isn't just for the presentation itself. Continue to make eye-contact as you answer questions. Look first to the person who asked, and then to other audience members as you continue your answer, so they also feel included (Pagana, 2010; Steele, 2009). Look back to the original questioner to check you have answered the question that was asked and in case there is a follow-up question.

What is your study about?

This question comes in many forms (e.g. "tell me more about your project?" or "what are you working on in the lab?"). The most important things for answering this question are: (a) to know your audience (the questioner) and (b) begin like your introduction with the big picture, then get narrow – only if they want to know more.

Usually, the answer to, "What is your study about?" should be only a couple of sentences long. Some people even call this the "elevator pitch:" a short two-minute summary that provides the most important information. Imagine running into the head of psychology in the elevator/lift, knowing he/she is exiting in ninety seconds. How could you quickly answer this question so that your answer is still useful and interesting?

When asked this question many students provide answers that are long-winded and really detailed. Answers like:

> I'm running a study on tasting tea and giving participants four cups of tea to drink. They rate them on a seven-point Likert scale from delicious, tasty, somewhat tasty, fine/neutral, somewhat untasty, untasty, to disgusting. I already tested twenty participants, but they are coming back to the lab for part two in May. They complete questionnaires about mood and stress on each visit. The cups of tea have different amount of sweeteners in them. One has no sweeter, one has five grams of sugar, one has ten grams of sugar, and one has organic honey. Oh, the sugar is also organic.

That is boring, and at the moment, no one cares how many grams of sugar you are using. Such information is very important for the method section, and it will be important to have a justification (5 grams is approximately 1 tsp).

Consider this answer:

> The study examines how taste preferences change under stress. I'm investigating this by giving students varying levels of sugar at the start of the academic year and during the exam period. As an additional control, students are completing a questionnaire about their stress levels. I expect that students will have a stronger preference for sugar under stress.

Doesn't that sound much more interesting? It also includes the hypothesis. It might be even better if I wasn't making this example up and could throw in some theory or science about why I expect that preference (but still keeping it brief). Now, if the questioner was just being nice she can smile, nod and change or stop the conversation, but if the questioner was genuinely curious – or you've sparked her curiosity – she can ask follow-up questions like, "How are you giving the sugar?" "How do you administer the taste test?" "Why do you think stress causes people to crave more sugar?" and especially "Do you think this generalizes beyond students and taking exams?"

To break it down, my better answer included:

- One sentence of a big picture (the ultimate goal, no jargon)
- One to two sentences on methods that mentioned the overall method and anything that could cause concern (How do you know they were really stressed?) but skipping the number of participants, skipping the number of trials, skipping the coding
- One sentence of hypothesis/specific outcome

You don't have to use this format, but it might help you start thinking.

If the person asking you has some background in psychology, you can use this to your advantage to avoid defining jargon the person likely knows. Simply saying "a seven-point Likert scale" is probably sufficient. The questioner can guess that the end points of the scale are delicious and disgusting. If you really don't know the questioner (maybe you gave a talk in your department and you think the person asking is a post-doc or maybe a faculty member), use your best guess and look for body language signs that the person wants to hear more.

Knowing how to give an "elevator pitch" is useful in a variety of careers and also at various stages of your research, from recruiting pilot participants to final presentation.

However, do ask your mentor if you will be required to give a longer response.

> "Approaching people and having the confidence to talk passionately about the lab and convincing parents it was worthwhile for their children to take time out of their days, travel and take part in our activities is a great skill as it involves a special kind of sales technique where you cannot be seen to be 'salesy' but still need to convince parents that giving up their time and allowing their children to come to a lab was the best option for them. It also helps with learning how to identify your audience and change your language and demeanor to suit the person you are speaking to."
>
> —Rosa, BSc
> Senior Program Manager (Charity Sector)

"Taking a large amount of information and ensuring it was succinct enough to deliver in a presentation helped me to see what the 'take-home' messages of my project were. Having a time limit helped me learn to balance providing enough information while also keeping the presenting interesting for the audience."

—Emilly, MSc
Research Assistant

TABLE 6.1

Here are some questions to ask yourself to prepare for presenting your study

Question	Consider
What is your research project about?	Elevator pitch (but do ask your supervisor if you will be asked to give a longer answer)
Why did you use this particular method?	Consider for each task/design decision
Why did you use this particular statistical test?	Consider for each test
If you were to do this project again, what would you do differently and why?	Different task? Different task parameters? Has new research come out that would have informed your design?
What is the theoretical contribution of your research project?	How do your findings (even if null results) change what we know about your broader topic? Have you provided additional evidence for or against an existing theory, and if so how?
What are the practical implications of your research project?	Why should other people outside your department or research area care about this? Do your results lead to possible recommendations for any nonacademic groups (teachers, drivers, smokers, doctors, parents, city council members)?
If you were continuing, what would your next project be?	What is the logical next thing to test?
Is there an alternative explanation for your findings?	Could another theory or a simple explanation based on something in your methods account for what you found? Do you have any evidence (perhaps additional analyses) that can demonstrate this alternative could, in fact, not account for your findings?
How is your research project different from [each key study you cite in your research area]?	Did you extend the findings of previous research? Do you have additional controls or trials that others do not have? Have you pitted different theoretical explanations against each other?

Do your PREP

One method you can use to structure your presentation but also to answer difficult questions is PREP (Brody, 2008): point, reason, example, point. First, recap your point (the big idea/contribution), then give the reason (this might be a theoretical justification in response to a question or background literature in the main talk), then give an example (in psychology this would be in the form of empirical results) and recap your point.

Transferring your presentation skills to job interviews

Many of these same principles for presentations you can use for job interviews. For example, you will want to have a clear, succinct elevator pitch (p. 169) answer ready for, "Tell me about your previous experience." If a panel is interviewing you, you will want to also make eye contact with those who didn't ask the question (as well as the person who did). You can also keep in mind that your interviewers will know you are likely nervous and will remember giving interviews themselves.

Transferable skills

Here are some situations where you might want to talk about the skills you learned during your research project in an interview.

"What skills make you qualified/well-suited for this position?"

A related question is "what are your strengths?" Think about the skills most relevant for the position and how you have already learned those or related skills.

- Computer skills: Consider your data entry, data analysis, presentation skills.
- Sales/people skills: Consider if you recruited participants, worked with others, liaised with other labs for resources, interviewed participants.
- Creativity: Did you create a new method for your study? Did you have to be creative in recruiting participants or hiding the real purpose of the task until later?
- Communication skills: Consider if you gave presentations, communicated with others, recruited participants (verbal communication). Also consider if you wrote procedures or other documents that others needed to follow or learn from (written communication).

- Strong work ethic: Did you ever go above and beyond working on your project?
- Handling finances: Consider if you coordinated payments for participants or if your computer skills are relevant.
- Record keeping: If you worked with humans you responsibly took care of consent forms or maybe other sensitive information (e.g. a database of potential participants).

"When have you taken initiative/been proactive?"

Was there a time with your study or for the lab when something wasn't ideal and you created a new method or procedure to deal with it? This can also be an opportunity to give your strong work ethic example.

"What are your weaknesses?"

Consider if there is something you learned about yourself while doing your project that you have tried to improve and demonstrate how you have worked on that skill.

> "It is vitally important to reflect on your achievements and also, more importantly, the times when you have not performed as you had hoped, or not achieved the desired result. It is a good idea to get into the habit of regularly reflecting as this is a valuable work and life skill. At work, this will demonstrate a commitment to continued professional development. Within your studies, an example of when it would be appropriate to reflect could be reflecting on why you have had an unproductive day, and how you can improve on this the next day. Or within research, there could be an opportunity to reflect on the skills used to recruit participants and how these could be utilized to maximum effect."
>
> —Sam, BSc
> Life Skills Recovery Worker (NHS)

There are many books, websites and other resources available to help you prepare for a job interview. Your university may even have a careers center, with dedicated staff there to help you. Also look for an alumni network that might help students and graduates connect with others who have chosen similar career paths. After months of conducting literature searches and evaluating how much weight to place on different things you read, you are well prepared to conduct research in the area of interviewing and the kinds of jobs or companies you are interested in.

Box 6.7: Continuing in psychology

By the time you finish your project, you may have discovered that you love research and do want to continue in psychology. The best, first place to go for advice in this area is to your supervisor and academic advisor. He or she will know how strong you are as a candidate (some fields <cough/clinical!/cough> are extremely competitive to get into) and if you should first seek more work experience by becoming an RA or if you should start working on your applications.

Faculty in your department may also have specific inside information that you might want to know now rather than later (and the kind of information you would never find looking at other departments online). For example, I know one professor who once announced he would not be taking any new PhD students because he already had five and didn't feel he could be a good mentor if he was spreading his attention among six students. If you had applied to work with him that year your application would have been rejected – and it would have nothing to do with you, your abilities or your academic record. Your faculty mentor might also know other things like, "Actually, that person is on the job market and wants to move to be closer to a spouse." Or "So-and-so has a reputation of being difficult to work with. Students in that lab publish several papers, but if you look, they never work with that person after they leave."

If you do prepare a research proposal or personal statement, consider re-reading Chapter 5 because many of the same ideas for clear writing apply to that kind of writing as well.

Transferring these skills

Being able to create easy-to-follow tables and graphs is a useful skill for any job that requires tracking something over time (e.g. patients admitted, payments received, new customers). Likewise, being able to give a good presentation is useful anytime you need to meet with other people to discuss the next steps or to pitch an idea. You might not necessarily always need to give a PowerPoint presentation, but you will likely need to remember not to be nervous, think of how to articulate your big idea in just a few sentences (i.e. elevator pitch) and answer questions in front of one or more people. If your job involves recruiting or meeting with potential customers (e.g. at an industry show), it may be helpful to keep in mind that most questions are genuinely requests for clarity. If you are making promotional or marking materials, the tips we discussed about creating PowerPoint slides (e.g. white space, font size, etc.) will also transfer to that medium.

Conclusions

Conducting research is complicated. Honestly, it's not really that difficult to repeat the same procedure over and over again when you are collecting data. Learn the procedure, practice and repeat N times. Probably a bit tedious by the end, but straightforward to learn.

But research is so much more than actually running your experiment. By conducting research you have learned to plan ahead and make decisions about how you will really analyze the data so you know how to enter it. You have learned to communicate your ideas clearly so one group of people will be willing to participate and another group will understand why you did what you did and why it was worth doing. You have honed skills related to how you manage your time, resources and large amounts of information. You may have also learned how to use complicated machines or get nonhuman animals to understand what you need them to do. Doing research well requires using a wide range of skills.

I hope this book has helped you learn some of these skills and answered some of the questions you may have had along the way. Fortunately, most of the skills you have mastered are skills you will be able to continue to use after you graduate, no matter if you continue in psychology or not. I'm very serious! Take another look:

But research is so much more than actually running your experiment. By conducting research you have learned to plan ahead and make decisions about how you will really analyze the data so you know how to enter it. You have learned to communicate your ideas clearly so one group of people will be willing to participate and another group will understand why you did what you did and why it was worth doing. You have honed skills related to how you manage your time, resources and large amounts of information. You may have also learned how to use complicated machines or

~~get nonhuman animals to understand what you need them to do.~~ Doing research well requires using a wide range of skills.

In a year or two or even more, if someone asks what you learned when you conducted your research project, I hope you don't only answer, "I learned some difference in [one variable] is related to/causes a difference in [another variable]." I hope you answer something like, "Wow, I learned so many skills – and I use them all the time."

References

American Psychological Association. (2010). *Publication Manual of the American Psychological Assocation: Sixth Edition*. Washington, DC: American Psychological Association.

Brody, M. (2008). *Speaking is an Audience-Centered Sport* (4th ed.). Jenkintown, PA: Career Skills Press.

Horst, J. S., Scott, E. J., & Pollard, J. P. (2010). The Role of Competition in Word Learning Via Referent Selection. *Developmental Science, 13*(5), 706–13. doi: 10.1111/j.1467-7687.2009.00926.x.

Pagana, K. D. (2010). *The Nurse's Communication Advantage: How Business Savvy Communication Can Advance Your Nursing Career*. Indianapolis, IN: SIGMA Theta Tau International.

Shakespeare, W. (1600). *The Tragedy of Hamlet, Prince of Denmark*.

Steele, W. R. (2009). *Presentation Skills 201: How to Take It to the Next Level as a Confident, Engaging Presenter*. Denver, CO: Outskirts Press.

Williams, S. E., & Horst, J. S. (2014). Goodnight Book: The Benefit of Sleep Consolidation on Word Learning via Storybooks. *Frontiers in Psychology, 5*(184), 1–12. doi: 10.3389/fpsyg.2014.00184.

Index

Note: Page numbers in *italics* indicate figures and tables.